Knowing the Body — the Fellowship of the Body of Christ

VISION - bread & cup means we are in the one fellowship - one Body
Fellowship is the flow of the divine life. I John 1:3 you may have fellowship
   Rev 22:1 flows is coming from the throne - NJ - if you are not in the flow
      yn are not in the NJ
by the Spirit, in the Spirit, of the Spirit - called "the fellowship of the H.
We need fellowship - blood circulation - does 2 things - carries nutrients
   to us + negative things away from us. Blood circulation carries
   problems away. We should keep the Spirit circulating.

I. the fellowship of the apostles (Acts 2:42) - the teaching is the element
   & realm of the fellowship. Teaching is the unveiling of GNTE re
   Christ + the Church; fellowship is the communion

Lord's Recovery:
   Lord desires to recover Christ as everything to us   1 Cor 1:9
      "   "   "   "   the oneness of the Body of Christ   John 17
                                                                    21-23 y
      "   "   "   "   the functioning of all the members
                    Eph 4:16, 1 Cor 14:4b, 26, 31

   (never visited regularly other localities: Gaithersburg, Beltsville, other HMs)
   lack of fellowship - gives enemy chance to come in
   best way to stay healthy "to receive more blood, give more blo

WITNESS LEE

The
Vision
of the
Age

Living Stream Ministry
Anaheim, California • www.lsm.org

First Edition, April 2003.

ISBN 0-7363-2258-2

Published by

Living Stream Ministry
2431 W. La Palma Ave., Anaheim, CA 92801 U.S.A.
P. O. Box 2121, Anaheim, CA 92814 U.S.A.

Printed in the United States of America

03 04 05 06 07 08 09 / 9 8 7 6 5 4 3 2 1

CONTENTS

PREFACE

This book is a translation of three messages given by Brother Witness Lee in March 1986 to the elders and co-workers in Taipei, Taiwan. These messages were not reviewed by the speaker.

CHAPTER ONE

VISION IN GOD'S ECONOMY

Prayer: Lord, we trust in Your precious blood. May Your blood cleanse us. We long to live in fellowship with You. We do not want any sin, any evil, or anything that is contrary to You to veil our inner being; we do not want to lose Your light, miss our fellowship with You, or forego our enjoyment of Your presence. Lord, be our sin offering and trespass offering. We do not want to have some religious activities or busy outward works while missing Your inner presence and not touching You. Lord, in such a training, keep us so that we would remain in fellowship with You and that we would touch Your heart's desire and Yourself. We want to know not only the objective words in the Bible, but Your subjective work within us, the work which You are doing in the church today. Lord, be gracious to us and speak to the depth of our being. We want to be taught and encouraged; but more than that, we want to know Your way and be preserved by You, gained by You, and sustained by You. May You grow within us, daily softening us, so that we would be truly mingled with You and be in one fellowship with You. May there be genuine growth within us, and may there be a broad pathway within us that will open all the doors in us.

Lord, in our sojourn on this earth, it is unavoidable that we come short and are defiled all the time. Do forgive us of all our shortcomings. Cleanse us of all our defilements. Save us, and remove all filthiness so that our mind, heart, and spirit, including our conscience, would be clear. Lord, may our fellowship here be a pure flow, clear as crystal, without any shadow or covering. Grant us an open sky; remove all veils. May both the speaker and the listeners be in one spirit. Whatever we would cover, may all of us touch the same thing and may all of us get into it and pursue after it in spirit. Lead us into You to receive Your cherishing, care, and supply so that we may experience the genuine growth. Lord, guide us to speak the same thing. We have no preconceived decisions; we only want to move according to Your Spirit. Speak to us again and again the words that are in Your heart. Amen.

THE NEED FOR VISION AMONG THE SERVING ONES

In this chapter we will first consider the kind of vision that a servant of the Lord should possess.

What Is a Vision?

Among the serving ones, the two most important groups of people are the elders and the co-workers. According to the Bible, a servant of the Lord must be governed by a vision. We have been speaking about this point for many years. From the first day the work began here in Taiwan, we have been speaking about vision. Over twenty years ago, this matter affected some young people. They felt that they had seen the vision, and they called themselves the "vision group." They condemned the elderly saints for not having any vision.

Whether or not a person understands a certain biblical term is an important matter. Even when a person understands a term, it is very important to know if he understands it correctly and accurately. Proverbs 29:18 says, "Where there is no vision, the people cast off restraint." This means that without a vision, the people will become loose, like wild horses in their untamed state. The clearest instance in the New Testament where the word *vision* is mentioned is in the case of Paul. In Acts 26:19, while he was defending himself before King Agrippa, he uttered this word: "I was not disobedient to the heavenly vision." In order to understand the meaning of the word *vision,* we have to understand the context of Paul's speaking in verses 4-23.

Prior to verse 19, Paul told us that he was once a zealous Judaizer, being zealous for the religion and traditions of his forefathers. He was so zealous that he could not tolerate any different teachings or beliefs among his fellow Jews. Yet at that time there was a group of Christians whose words, teachings, actions, and works were different from the ordinances and the very root of Paul's Jewish religion. Paul's native town of Tarsus was at the crossroads between Asia Minor and Syria; it was a hub of communication and a historically famous academic town, a city of culture. In Tarsus there was a Greek school, and Paul received the highest education there. At the same time, he joined one of the strictest sects of Judaism and became a Pharisee, sitting under the most famous teacher, Gamaliel. We can see that he was a learned, ambitious, active, and aspiring person.

While he was yet a young man, he received authority from the chief priests in the Jewish religion to put many believers into prison. He even cast a vote to condemn them and to put them to death. Many times he persecuted the believers in the synagogues and compelled them to blaspheme. He was exceedingly enraged at them and persecuted them as far as the Gentile cities. He even requested a letter from the chief priests and took the lead to put into bondage all those who called on the name of the Lord. But while he was on the way to Damascus, the Lord met him and said to him, "Saul, Saul, why are you persecuting Me? It is hard for you to kick against the goads" (v. 14). Paul asked, "Who are You, Lord?" The Lord said, "I am Jesus, whom you persecute" (v. 15). Then the Lord told him that He had chosen him to be a minister and a witness both of the things in which he had seen Him and of the things in which He would appear to him. He would send Paul to the people and the Gentiles to open their eyes, to turn them from darkness to light and from the authority of Satan to God that they might receive forgiveness of sins and an inheritance among those who have been sanctified by faith. After testifying of these things, Paul concluded by saying, "Therefore...I was not disobedient to the heavenly vision" (v. 19). When Paul was serving God in the Jewish religion, he was serving by tradition, not by vision, but from the day the Lord met him, called him, and chose him on the way to Damascus, he became a man with a vision. From that time onward, his service was governed by that vision.

Concerning the word *vision,* our emphasis is not on its Old Testament meaning but on what Paul said in Acts 26:19. Of course, we can never ascertain a truth in the Bible by one verse alone. Every truth in the Bible requires the entire Bible for its explanation. This is like the various organs of the body; none can survive alone. They need the entire body to act as their support. In the same way, every truth must have the entire "body" as its support. The entire Bible is the whole "body," the supporting structure. In order to understand what the word *vision* means, we have to consider the entire Bible.

Many Christians have read the biography of Hudson Taylor. The writer told us clearly that while Mr. Taylor was young, he felt that he had to go to China for the gospel. He first joined a mission and went to northern Fukien for the gospel. Later, one day while he was back in England on furlough, he went to the seashore to spend some time alone with the Lord. As he gazed at the ocean, he felt that his eyes were brought across the seas to catch a glimpse of the interior parts of China, and he saw four hundred million dying souls. He felt that the Lord was calling him to consecrate himself entirely to those people and to send the gospel to the interior of China. Right there he accepted this charge and commission. Such a charge and commission became Mr. Taylor's "vision." Immediately he shared what he saw with the Christians whom he was acquainted with. Many responded to his word, and the China Inland Mission was formed. In the following forty to fifty years, hundreds and thousands of people were sent to the interior parts of China to preach the gospel.

It is debatable whether what Mr. Taylor saw can be considered a vision of the age. Of course the vast China needed the preaching of the gospel. From this viewpoint, Mr. Taylor indeed received a commission, and it was indeed a vision. Yet it is questionable whether or not that is the vision that God has for this age. Concerning the matter of vision, we must come back to the Bible.

GOD'S VISIONS
THROUGH AN OUTLINE OF THE OLD TESTAMENT

From Adam to Samuel

The Bible has sixty-six books. The Old Testament begins

with God's creation, or Adam's creation, and spans four thousand years until the birth of the Lord Jesus. The first two volumes of Level One of *Truth Lessons* give us a description and an outline of the Old Testament. The purpose of such a description is to show us the various visions God gave to men throughout the ages. We have to see that in every age, God gives only one vision to man. In Adam is seen God's redemption. In Abel is seen God's way of redemption. In Enosh is seen man's need for God and man's calling upon Him to enjoy His riches. In Enoch is seen a redeemed one walking with God on the pathway of redemption. In Noah is seen one who walked with God and worked with God to build the ark to meet the need of that generation.

Then in Abraham is seen God's calling, God's promise, justification by faith, the living by faith, and the living in fellowship with God. In Isaac is seen the inheriting of grace and the rest and enjoyment. In Jacob is seen God's selection, the transformation in life, and the maturity in life. In Joseph is seen the reigning aspect of the maturity in life. Following this, we see different things in Moses, Aaron, Joshua, and the judges. In Samuel we see the voluntarily consecrated Nazarite replacing the ordained priests, ending the age of the judges, and bringing in the kingdom age. In Acts 13 Paul mentioned this period of history and spoke of God's leading of the Israelites out of Egypt. Through Joshua He led them into the land of Canaan and divided unto them the good land for their inheritance. After this, He appointed judges from among them until the time of Samuel, at which time He ushered in David. This period lasted about four hundred fifty years.

The Way of Reckoning in the Age of the Judges

We have to learn to interpret the Bible with the Bible. The Life-study trainings emphasize life; they do not pay that much attention to history, genealogies, and dates. This is why they give detailed explanations of the things of life but spend little time to explain history and dates. In Acts 13:20 Paul says, "And after these things, for about four hundred and fifty years, He gave them judges until Samuel the prophet." There are at least two or three authoritative interpretations of this verse. It is hard to ascertain the exact number of years in this case. However, since this period of time has much to do with the vision given at that time, we have to study the matter in depth. How do these four hundred fifty years come about?

First Kings 6:1 says, "Then in the four hundred eightieth year after the children of Israel had come forth out of the land of Egypt, in the fourth year of his [Solomon's] reign over Israel..." The Israelites were in the wilderness for forty years. After this, Joshua led for twenty-five years. Then there was the time of the judges, which lasted until the time of Samuel. The four hundred fifty years that Paul spoke of in Acts 13:20 surely include all these events. David's reign lasted for forty years, and afterwards there was the reign of Solomon. If we add up these numbers, we can see one thing: Paul's word in Acts 13 does not take Saul's years into account because at the time he was king, there was a rival, which was David. We can say that during that period of time there was no properly appointed king from God to unite the whole nation of Israel. Strictly speaking, before the Israelites were united as one nation, they were still in the age of the judges.

Although Saul was appointed by God to be king, in God's eyes his words did not count; only Samuel's words counted. Samuel held both the position of a prophet and a judge. At that time, outwardly Saul was king, but in reality, in God's eyes, Samuel was still functioning as a judge. As for David, he was anointed early on, but at the beginning it was neither his words nor Saul's words that counted, but Samuel's words. Even after David became king, his first seven and a half years were not reckoned in Paul's four hundred fifty years because at that time the house of Saul was not yet removed; Saul's son Ishbosheth was still king in Mahanaim (2 Sam. 2:8-11). In the eyes of God, that was still the age of the judges.

Based on the above, we can make a clear conclusion: The age of the judges was terminated only after David became king over all of Israel. David unified the entire nation of Israel and was officially recognized as king in Jerusalem. After this there was no more confusion or disturbances in the land. This lasted for thirty-three years. According to 1 Kings 6:1, from the time of the exodus to the fourth year of Solomon were four hundred eighty years. Subtracting from that the last thirty-three years of David's reign and the first three years of Solomon's reign, we have four hundred forty-four years left. This somewhat matches Paul's word in Acts 13:20: "For about four hundred and fifty years." The difference of the two is only six years. This is why Paul used the word *about.*

Within the period of the time of the judges, which lasted approximately four hundred fifty years, was the reign of Saul, which lasted forty years. But God did not recognize him as king. The reason for this is that he did not serve as king according to a vision. Samuel, on the other hand, was recognized as a judge because he served with a vision. This can be proven by the fact that the age of the judges did not end until the termination of the ministry of Samuel. Of course, the final termination of the age of the judges began with the reign of David in Jerusalem. The period of proper kingship does not include the first seven and a half years of David's reign. In God's eyes, the throne was empty at that time because there were still contenders for the throne, and the nation was under the turmoil of war. During those seven and a half years, the Israelites did not serve according to a vision. Although both Saul and David (during his first seven and a half years of reign) were kings, the only one who served according to a vision was Samuel, who served as a judge.

SERVING GOD ACCORDING TO THE VISION OF THE AGE

We must be clear that in every age there is the vision of that age. We have to serve God according to the vision of the age. Consider the age of Noah. When we read the record of the Bible, it appears as if Noah's family, including himself, his wife, his three children, and their wives were the only ones who were serving God. Can we believe that at that time there were actually only eight people serving God, and the rest were worshipping idols and not serving God? Perhaps we have never thought about this matter. Whether or not others were serving God, one thing is certain: They were not part of those who built the ark. For this very reason their service was not recognized by God.

Perhaps some people will ask whether at the time Noah was busily building the ark there was not a single person on earth who feared God. We can deduce from historical data that at the time of Noah it is quite possible that his one family with eight people were not the only ones serving and worshipping God. The ancient Chinese were serving and worshipping also at that time. Their way of worship was in many ways similar to that of men in the Old Testament. Confucius was five hundred years prior to Christ. He once said, "To sin against heaven is unforgivable." In the parable of the prodigal son in Luke 15, the prodigal said to his father when he returned home, "I have sinned against heaven" (v. 21). In ancient times, both the East and the West considered "heaven" a symbol for God. The reason for this is that whenever men lifted their heads heavenward, they thought about God. We can assume that in the ancient times many people sought after God and had some knowledge of God. They served God according to the knowledge they had of God. Yet we must realize that though so many people were serving, only Noah and his family of eight served with a vision, and only their service was acceptable to God.

MOVING UNDER A VISION AND FOLLOWING THOSE WHO HAVE THE VISION

When Jesus of Nazareth came, He also served God, and a group of Galilean fishermen followed Him as His disciples. In the eyes of man, these Galileans were just like little naughty children. Outwardly, Jesus was a Galilean; He did not move away from Nazareth the first thirty years of His life, and He received no formal education in serving God. Yet at the age of thirty He started a ministry, and a group of "ignorant" people followed Him. Even some women ministered to His needs. They followed the Lord Jesus for three and a half years. What do you think the Pharisees, chief priests, scribes, and elders thought of them at that time? Among these men were fishermen, tax-collectors, and relatives of the Lord Jesus. There was even a woman who was once possessed with seven demons. Did they not seem to be children at play when they claimed that they were serving God?

At that time among the Jews, there was still a magnificent temple. It was built over a period of forty years. The Levites were divided into twenty-four orders and were offering sacrifices and ministering according to their orders. They were either taking care of the utensils, slaying the animals, or offering the sacrifices such as the daily burnt offerings and sin offerings and the weekly Sabbath offerings on the brass altar. In the eyes of man, such services were indeed proper and dignified, but were they carried out under a vision? We are all very clear that the services of the priests in the temple were not carried out under a vision; they were carried out by tradition. It was the Lord Jesus and those who were following Him who were serving under a vision and whose service was pleasing to God.

The followers of the Lord Jesus were a blessed people. Among them was Peter, who was also a leader and one who took the lead to say foolish things. There was Mary the Magdalene who was once possessed with seven demons. There was also the other Mary, who loved the Lord fervently and who broke the flask of alabaster worth thirty pieces of silver to anoint the Lord Jesus. Outwardly they were all blindly following the Lord because the Lord Jesus was the only One who had the vision. Peter, James, John, Mary, and all the others did not receive that vision. Yet they were clear that the Lord's way was right and were determined to follow Him. When the Lord turned to the east, they followed to the east. When the Lord turned to the west, they followed to the west. When the Lord went to the sea, they followed Him to the sea. When the Lord went to the mountain, they followed Him to the mountain. When the Lord was in Galilee, they followed Him in Galilee. When the Lord went to Jerusalem, they followed Him to Jerusalem. They were resolved in their heart that as long as they followed the Lord, nothing would go wrong.

In John 11 Lazarus was dying. When the Lord learned about this, He did not do anything. After two days the Lord told the disciples that He would go to see Lazarus. The disciples said to Him, "The Jews were just now seeking to stone You, and You are going there again?" (v. 8). The Lord answered, "Our friend Lazarus has fallen asleep; but I am going that I may wake him out of sleep" (v. 11). Verses 1-16 show that the disciples were truly following in a blind way. They were not at all clear what they were doing, yet they followed and went anyway. Perhaps in the eyes of men this is blind following, yet this kind of following pleases God, and this kind of following is done with a vision. They did not receive any vision individually, but the One whom they were following had the vision, and that was enough. As long as they were acting according to the One who had the vision, they were right in the eyes of God.

GOD'S VISIONS
THROUGH AN OUTLINE OF THE NEW TESTAMENT

Today many Christians criticize us, saying, "You are too proud. How can you negate all the denominations and all the Christians and say that only you have the vision?" Some brothers and sisters on occasion have been asked by others, "You say that the pastors are wrong, the pope is wrong, and everybody is wrong. Are you the only people that are not wrong? Are you the only ones who are right in following what you are following?" I believe sometimes such winds would even cause you to question yourselves. However, if we are clear about the vision in the Bible, we will have the confidence to say that we are indeed those who serve by following a vision.

The Service of Peter and His Companions

In the book of Acts, after the Lord's ascension, Peter and later Paul continued to serve in the ministry. In Acts 5, while Peter was ministering, the Jewish synagogue rose up to oppose the apostles and put them into prison (vv. 17-32). But the Lord's angel at night opened the doors of the prison and, leading them out, told them to stand in the temple and speak to the people all the words of this life. At daybreak the chief priests called together the Sanhedrin and asked for the apostles to be brought to them. When the officers arrived, they found the prison locked with all security and the guards standing at the doors, but when they opened the doors, they found no one inside. While they were utterly perplexed, someone came and reported to them, "Behold, the men whom you put in the prison are standing in the temple and teaching the people" (v. 25). Then the captain with the officers went away and brought the apostles to the Sanhedrin to be tried. After the Sanhedrin listened to the apostles, it wanted to do away with them. One Pharisee among them, Gamaliel, a teacher of the law honored by all the people, stood up and said, "Withdraw from these men and leave them alone; for should this counsel or this work be of men, it will be overthrown; but if it is of God, you will not be able to overthrow them, lest you be found to be even fighters against God" (vv. 38-39). Gamaliel's word was correct, but this does not mean that he had the vision. The only ones who had the vision were the apostles who were imprisoned and the simple ones who were following them.

In Acts 12 Herod began to persecute the church. He killed James and put Peter into prison. A large group of women gathered in the house of Mary, the mother of John, to pray for Peter. In the night the Lord's angel opened the door of the prison and took Peter out. Peter went to the house of Mary and knocked at the door. A maiden came to answer (vv. 1-13). In the eyes of the Sanhedrin, the chief priests, and the Pharisees, these women were foolish. They would not go to the proper temple and would not abide by the tradition of their forefathers; they chose to follow a group of Galilean fishermen and mingle with them. Could it be that all of their forefathers were wrong? Could it be that David, Isaiah, and all the others were wrong and that these Galileans alone were right? Moreover, they had even been imprisoned. Yet the women were still praying for them and following them. It seems that they were too foolish.

Here we see two groups of people. The larger group was the Jewish religionists. The smaller group was those who followed Peter and the other Galileans in a simple way. Both groups were serving God, but whose service was under a vision? I am afraid that we have never thought about this matter. We have to see that not only was Peter's service under a vision, but even the simple ones who followed him were serving under a vision.

The Service of Paul and His Companions

In Acts 11 Barnabas took Paul along with him in his service and brought him to Antioch (vv. 25-26). This was something done according to the vision. In chapter thirteen we find that one day the Holy Spirit spoke to those who were serving in Antioch, saying, "Set apart for Me now Barnabas and Saul for the work to which I have called them" (v. 2). Here the Scripture puts Barnabas first. This shows that he was the leader. In recording their journey, the Bible puts Barnabas's name first and Paul's name second. When they came to Pisidian Antioch, however, and the need arose for someone to speak in the synagogue on the Sabbath, Barnabas had nothing to say. At that time, Saul, who was called Paul, stood up, motioned with his hand, and began to preach the gospel and pour out his speaking like a torrent (vv. 16-41). From that time onward, the Bible reverses the order of the two men; it begins to address them as "Paul and Barnabas." This shows that at that time the vision turned to Paul.

In Acts 15 after Paul and Barnabas returned from the conference in Jerusalem, they had the burden to revisit the cities in which they previously preached and see the brothers again. At that juncture, Barnabas voiced his opinion; he wanted to bring Mark, his cousin, along with him. Paul disagreed, the two had a contention, and they separated from each other. Barnabas took Mark and went another way, while Paul took Silas with him (vv. 36-40). From that time onward, the book of Acts has no more record of Barnabas. We believe that though Barnabas was still serving, his service was no longer governed by the vision. From that time, the ones who were serving under the vision were Paul and Silas, the one Paul had chosen.

Serving by Following the Leadership of Those Who Have the Vision

The Example of Aquila and Priscilla

At the beginning of Acts 18, we are told that through his tentmaking Paul gained a couple, Aquila and Priscilla. Immediately they joined Paul in his vision and commingled with him in his service. Thereafter, there were meetings in this couple's house continually. When they were in Rome, the church in Rome met in their house. When they went to Ephesus, the church in Ephesus met in their house (Rom. 16:5a; 1 Cor. 16:19b). Paul praised them for risking their necks for his life (Rom. 16:4). Not only was Paul grateful to them, but all the churches in the Gentile world were thankful to them. The service of Aquila and Priscilla was a service that followed after Paul. Hence, their service was a service under the vision.

The Case of Apollos

At the end of Acts 18, there appeared a man named Apollos. Was Apollos's service under the vision? It is not safe to say that it was not, for "he was powerful in the Scriptures" (v. 24). He knew the Bible very well, but while he was ministering and working in Corinth, he created some problems. After he left, a division arose in the church in Corinth. Some said that they were of Apollos, while others said that they were of Cephas or of Paul. Another group of people thought that they were superior; they did not consider themselves as belonging to anyone. They claimed that they were of Christ (1 Cor. 1:12). Because of this problem, Paul said in 1 Corinthians 16:12, "And concerning our brother Apollos, I urged him many times to come to you with the brothers; yet it was not at all his desire to come now, but he will come when he has opportunity." This means that Paul wanted to go to Corinth, and he wanted Apollos to go with him to solve the problem of division in the church in Corinth. The strange thing is that although Paul "urged him many times," "it was not at all [Apollos's] desire to come now." The reason Apollos gave was that the opportunity was not there. This was why he would only come when he had "opportunity."

Today we all have to admit that Paul was a very spiritual man. Since such a spiritual person had said, "I urged him many times to come to you," we have to believe that his urging was not of the flesh but of the spirit. Perhaps some may ask, "Does this mean that Apollos was not spiritual?" Many would answer, "Of course Apollos was spiritual. Otherwise, why would some in Corinth have claimed that they were of Apollos?" The Bible clearly says that Apollos was powerful in the

Scriptures and was an eloquent man. Even Paul affirmed
Apollos by saying that he planted but Apollos watered. It is
difficult to say that the one who plants is under the vision but
the one who waters is not under the vision. Therefore, we can
at most say that Paul was more spiritual than Apollos. We
cannot say that Apollos was not spiritual and that he was not
under the vision.

The Pattern of Timothy and Titus

Today in Christianity, many Christians claim that they
are spiritual, but they do not like to listen to others. Even if
Paul were here, they might not listen to him. This attitude
has even found its way to us. It seems that in a way we are
also "spiritual." Sometimes we have a feeling about a certain
matter, but we can only say to the brothers, "I urge you to do
this. Perhaps you can pray to the Lord about it." Strictly
speaking, this condition is not too normal. If we study the
book of Acts and the Epistles of Paul, we can see that many
times Paul pointedly told people to do certain things. In
2 Timothy 4, Paul directed people to do a number of things.
He told Timothy, "Be diligent to come to me quickly....Take
Mark and bring him with you, for he is useful to me for the
ministry. But Tychicus I have sent to Ephesus. The cloak
which I left in Troas with Carpus, bring when you come...Be
diligent to come before winter" (vv. 9-13, 21). When Paul
charged Timothy in this way, Timothy did not say, "It is not at
all my desire to come now, because the weather is somewhat
cold, but I will come when I have opportunity." No, he acted
accordingly, following Paul's instruction.

In the same way, when Paul asked Titus to remain in
Crete, Titus remained. When he asked Titus to come to him at
Nicopolos, Titus obeyed. When he sent Titus to Corinth, Titus
went accordingly (Titus 1:5; 3:12; 2 Cor. 7:6-7). In 1 Timothy
1:3, Paul told Timothy, "Even as I exhorted you...to remain in
Ephesus." Paul told Timothy to stay behind in Ephesus, and
Timothy stayed behind. We cannot find a trace where Paul
exhorted Timothy in the way of saying, "Timothy, for the sake
of those who are teaching differently in Ephesus, I feel that
you should stay behind and consider the situation. Please

pray to the Lord to see whether or not this is the Lord's will."
Nor can we find Timothy answering, "Good, I will pray and
see. If it is the Lord's will, I will stay behind." Acts 17:15 says,
"And those who conducted Paul brought him as far as Athens;
and receiving a command for Silas and Timothy to come to
him as quickly as possible, they went off." Acts 18:5 says,
"Both Silas and Timothy came down from Macedonia." They
all obeyed immediately after they received Paul's command.
No one said, "Sorry, I have to pray a little and see if this is the
Lord's leading."

SERVING ACCORDING TO
THOSE WHO HAVE THE VISION
BEING TO SERVE UNDER THE VISION

We see clearly from the revelation of the New Testament
that when the Lord Jesus was on earth, He was acting under
the vision. Outside His leading there was no vision. Others
might have been in tradition or knowledge. Gamaliel was
very knowledgeable; he was very familiar with God's principles, but he was not under the vision. His speaking was not
under the vision; it was a speaking that was merely words of
knowledge. After the Lord's ascension, it was Peter and his
co-workers who were under the vision. We are not saying that
Peter had one vision and John, James, and the other apostles
had another vision. There was only one vision, which was the
vision of Peter. This vision became the vision of his followers.
When Paul was raised up in his ministry, he received a vision
that touched the heavens, the earth, and Paradise (2 Cor.
12:2-4). Although Paul had many co-workers, no one except
him saw any other vision. They all had one vision, which was
the vision that Paul saw.

There is great controversy in Christianity about this
matter of one vision for one age. However, God's Word reveals
to us clearly that in every age there is only one vision. At the
time of Abel, Cain did not worship an idol and he did not
build a shrine. He was doing the same thing that Abel was
doing, offering a sacrifice to God. Under the vision, however,
Abel offered a sacrifice that was acceptable to God, while
Cain offered his sacrifice apart from the vision. If you were

born in the age of Abel, you would have had to take the way of Abel; otherwise, you would have been off from the vision and in the way of Cain. At the time of Enosh, one man was under the vision, and he called on the name of the Lord. Other people might have feared God according to other ways, but such fear was not according to the vision. In the same way, at the time of Noah there were more than eight people who feared God; there might have been a hundred or even a thousand people who feared God. They might not have sinned as others did; they might even have been serving in some way. Yet their service was not governed by a vision. Noah's family of eight people, by serving after Noah's pattern, became servants who served according to a vision. What Noah saw became what they saw.

The vision that Noah saw was the vision of the ark. To man this was very peculiar and unthinkable. How can a person give up everything that he is doing and spend all his time building an ark? The building took one hundred twenty years (Gen. 6:3). During those one hundred twenty years, Noah was, on the one hand, preaching the word of righteousness and, on the other hand, building the ark (2 Pet. 2:5). To others he was wasting his effort and his money; he was too foolish. When the one hundred twenty years were about to end, there was still no sign of any rain from heaven. Yet while men were saying "peace and security," and while they were eating, drinking, marrying, and giving in marriage, the flood of destruction suddenly came, as birth pangs come suddenly to a woman with child (Matt. 24:38-39; 1 Thes. 5:3). In the end, only Noah's family entered the ark and was saved.

We find the same principle in the New Testament. God's work in the New Testament is to produce and build up the church. This vision was given to Paul. This is why once Paul came on the scene, Peter's ministry faded away. When Peter was old, he said, "Our beloved brother Paul, according to the wisdom given to him, wrote to you, as also in all his letters, speaking in them concerning these things, in which some things are hard to understand, which the unlearned and unstable twist, as also the rest of the Scriptures, to their own destruction" (2 Pet. 3:15-16). This means that even the aged

Peter had to submit to the vision of Paul. He acknowledged that Paul's word was as precious as the Old Testament Scriptures and that believers should take heed to it.

Based on this, the names of all those who did not join themselves to Paul's vision were eventually dropped from the record of the Bible. For example, Barnabas was the one who initiated Paul into the service, but because he contended with Paul, his name was eventually dropped from the Bible. Apollos was very capable at expounding the Bible, but 1 Corinthians 16 records that he told Paul that it was not at all his desire to go to Corinth and that he would go when he had opportunity. After this, the Bible no longer mentions anything about him. Barnabas was zealous in his service, and Apollos was capable in his exposition of the Bible, but God did not use them anymore because their service was no longer under the vision. This is a very sober matter.

TO SERVE UNDER THE VISION MEANING TO SERVE ACCORDING TO THE REVELATION OF THE BIBLE

The Bible shows us clearly that in every age God only gives the vision of the age to one man. We cannot find in the Bible that there were two visions in any age. What about those men who came after the apostles' time? How did they serve God according to the proper vision? Today Paul is gone. If we are to serve God today, what is our vision? Today the inhabited world is much larger than at the time of Noah; there are more people today. There are over one billion Christians all over the six continents of the world. They come from different denominations such as the Catholic Church and the Protestant churches. In the Protestant churches there are the Anglican Church, the Lutheran Church, the Methodist Church, the Baptist Church, and the Presbyterian Church. Among all these churches and all these Christians, who are the ones who are serving according to the vision? We can ask ourselves the same question: Are we those who are serving according to the vision, and if so, what is our vision?

Concerning this matter of following the vision, many Christians do not act according to the truth. Rather, they act according to their own taste and preferences. Some join our meetings because they think that the brothers and sisters here are very zealous; they love the Lord and the messages are good. This is the reason they join our meetings. Formerly, they only knew about attending "Sunday morning services." When they hear that we go to "church meetings," they also change their terminology and talk about attending "church meetings." Still very few believers are clear about what it is to meet and serve according to the vision. All of you here are elders and co-workers. It is important that you consider this matter carefully. What is our vision? What is the vision that is governing our service? We cannot answer this question in a general way with only some spiritual terminology. Our answer must be based on a solid foundation.

The Completion of the Divine Revelation

At the time of Abel, not a single book of the Bible had been written. It was fourteen hundred years after Abel, at the time of Moses, that the Pentateuch was completed. However, even at the time of Moses, God's revelation was still in the process of development; it was not yet complete. The vision that Moses saw was not enough to completely govern those who came after him. When we come to the New Testament, we find Paul saying that he became a minister to the church according to the stewardship that God had entrusted to him for the completion of the word of God (Col. 1:25). Around A.D. 94, three decades after Paul's martyrdom, the apostle John was raised up to do a mending work. He wrote the Gospel of John, the Epistles of John, and the book of Revelation. After these books were written, the revelation of God was fully completed. This is why at the end of Revelation John said, "If anyone adds to them [the words of the prophecy of this scroll], God will add to him the plagues which are written in this scroll" (22:18). This means that the apostle John's book of Revelation completes the entire revelation of God. The book of Revelation is indeed the ultimate consummation of God's revelation because Paul did not mention anything about the new heavens and the new earth, and Peter only mentioned them briefly (2 Pet. 3:13). Only the book of Revelation speaks about them in detail. This shows us clearly that by the time the apostle

John finished the book of Revelation, the biblical revelation had reached its ultimate consummation. This then becomes the vision and basis of our service today.

From the time of the apostles until today, for two thousand years, all the servants of the Lord who serve according to the revelation of the Bible serve according to the vision. This is the standard and the basis of our service. After the apostles passed away, servants of the Lord were raised up in every age. They argued, fought, and debated over whose service should be considered the genuine and right service. The verdict on such considerations should be based on the standard of the revelation as revealed in the Bible.

The Example of the Lord Jesus

Today, God's revelation is already put into writing. It is recorded in the Bible and is no longer something abstract. This is a very important matter. When the Lord Jesus spoke on the earth, He would say, "As the Scripture said" (John 7:38). Even while He was being tempted and was arguing with the devil, He said, "It is written" (Matt. 4:4, 7, 10). He did not speak according to any personal feeling within Him. This means that the divine revelation upon which He based His speaking is veritable; it is written in black and white and is not abstract at all. When He debated with the Pharisees, He quoted the Old Testament Scriptures. On the Sabbath day, when He took His disciples across the grainfields, the disciples picked ears of grain and ate. The Pharisees interrogated Him, and He answered, saying, "Have you not read what David did when he became hungry, and those who were with him; how he entered into the house of God, and they ate the bread of the presence, which was not lawful for him to eat, nor for those who were with him, except for the priests only?" (Matt. 12:3-4). During the final six days of His earthly journey, when He went up to Jerusalem and was questioned by the Pharisees, Sadducees, elders, and chief priests, He answered with the words of the Bible: "It is written....Have you never read?...Have you never read in the Scriptures?... Have you not read that which was spoken to you by God?" (Matt. 21:13, 16, 42; 22:31). This shows us clearly that the

Lord argued and justified Himself according to the revelation that was written down at the time.

The Example of the Apostles

In the book of Acts, both the apostles Peter and Paul spoke in the way of a defense. The first message that Peter delivered on the day of Pentecost was a defense based extensively on the Scriptures. He quoted the prophet Joel and proclaimed that Jesus of Nazareth, whom the people had crucified on the cross, had been raised up by God. This was what David referred to in Psalm 16. Moreover, as David prophesied in Psalm 110, God had exalted this Jesus to His right hand. Paul also wrote his Epistle to the Romans in the way of an argument based on the Old Testament. Someone said once that in order to be a good lawyer, one has to study the book of Romans thoroughly because this book contains the most perfect reasonings and the highest arguments.

STUDYING AND SERVING ACCORDING TO
THE REVELATION OF THE BIBLE

With the truth of the Bible as our guiding principle, we can study and examine all the denominations and sects that we find today. From this perspective, Catholicism is far off the mark. Surely Catholicism is not governed by the vision. The Anglican Church takes as its head the queen, who may not be saved at all. It considers all British citizens members of the Anglican Church by birth, whether or not they are believers and have been baptized. This clearly shows that the Anglican Church is not under the vision either. If we examine and compare all the other denominations, free groups, and charismatic organizations, we will see that none of them is serving fully according to the complete biblical revelation.

We should ask how high the standard of the revelation is which these groups hold. For example, we cannot say that Catholicism is a hundred percent contrary to the biblical revelation. At least it acknowledges one God, and it acknowledges that Jesus Christ is the Son of God. In the Catholic Church there are some truths, but their standard is too low. In the same way, we have to admit that many people in the

Protestant churches do expound the Bible. There are even Bible schools that teach people the truths of the Bible, but whether they see the revelation in the Bible and whether they are clear about God's vision are other questions altogether. We cannot say that as long as people have the Bible they have the revelation or are acting according to the vision. It is very possible that they merely hold the Bible in their hands; they have not released the vision and revelation contained in the Bible. Hence, we have to recognize some basic principles. First, we must be governed by the revelation contained in the Bible. Second, the standard of such revelation must be sufficiently high; it must be up to the standard of the divine revelation.

THE LORD'S RECOVERY BEING UNDER THE VISION OF THE DIVINE REVELATION

The knowledge and discovery of divine revelation develop and advance with the ages. Today we are not in the age of Martin Luther. We are not in the age of Zinzendorf or the age of John Wesley. At the time of the Reformation in the 1520s, when Luther was raised up, anyone who wanted to serve under a vision had to join himself to Luther. In the seventeenth century, anyone who wanted to serve under a vision had to join himself to Madam Guyon. In the eighteenth century, anyone who wanted to serve under a vision had to join himself to Zinzendorf. Even John Wesley received help from Zinzendorf. In the nineteenth century, J. N. Darby took the lead among the Brethren, and the vision was with him. In the twentieth century, the vision came to us.

I am not "selling" myself here, but I would like to make a declaration. I began my relationship with the Lord's recovery in 1925. I fully agreed with the Lord's recovery, but during the first seven and a half years I was not in the Lord's recovery but in the Brethren assembly. It was in 1932 that I officially joined the Lord's recovery. Now, fifty-four years have passed. During the past sixty years, according to my observation and based on my knowledge of the Bible, my experience as a Christian, and my study of Christianity's history and its present condition, I can say with full confidence that the Lord's recovery is serving under the vision. There is no doubt about this.

This is not all. During these fifty-four years that I have been in the Lord's recovery, I have seen many people both in the northern and southern parts of China who had high moral standards and noble characters, who had learned deep lessons in life, and whose spiritual condition was good. When they passed through the Lord's recovery or met with us for a few years and then left, invariably they found their spiritual service fading and faltering. This is an amazing thing. Those who have never touched the Lord's recovery can still somewhat go on, but those who have come and then left invariably find their end less than desirable. There is not one exception. This proves that the recovery bears the vision that the Lord has entrusted to this age.

At the time of Noah, the vision was to build the ark. At that time anyone who was not building the ark was not serving according to the vision. At the time of Paul, the vision was to preach the gospel and to build up the church. Anyone at that time who was not serving according to this vision was off the mark. This included such men as Apollos, who was capable at expounding the Bible, and Barnabas, who was zealous for his service. What is our vision today? Today in 1986, our vision is also to "build the ark." The way to build this ark is to preach the gospel, set up home meetings, teach the truth, and have everyone prophesy. All those who do not practice these four things are not serving according to the vision. Perhaps you expound the Bible, and perhaps you serve very zealously, but your service is not "building the ark." Such service will not be acceptable to God.

SERVING ACCORDING TO THE VISION
THAT THE LORD HAS GIVEN US TODAY

I hope that all the brothers and sisters attending the full-time training will read this chapter so that they will see this matter clearly. We are not trying to dictate to everybody, and we are not congratulating ourselves behind closed doors. We are saying this based on the movement of history and the pure revelation of the Bible. Look around at the entire situation of Christianity today. Where are the revelation and the vision? We have the same Bible in our hands, but some people have no light even after they have read it a hundred times. In the Lord's recovery, every page, every verse, even every sentence, and every word shines with revelation and light. I believe that outside the Lord's recovery it is hard to hear a word about Apollos like what is recorded in this chapter. The reason for this is that there is no light. If we study the letter of the Bible, we may conclude that Apollos was not too short. In 1 Corinthians 3 Paul said that Apollos watered, but in the same verse he told the Corinthians that he was the one who planted (v. 6). Whether or not there is a waterer is not that important, but the planter is indispensable (cf. Mark 4:26-28). Although Paul was humble in pointing out Apollos's distinction, in the same verse he added, "According to the grace of God given to me, as a wise master builder I have laid a foundation, and another builds upon it....For another foundation no one is able to lay besides that which is laid..." (1 Cor. 3:10-11). This means that anyone who does not build upon Paul's foundation is not serving according to the vision. In the eyes of man, this is too presumptuous, but Paul was not apologetic at all. He said that he was a wise master builder. He had given everyone the blueprint of the building, and he was supervising the building work. The word "master builder" here is *architekton* in Greek. It denotes a person who has the blueprint and builds and supervises the building according to the blueprint. The anglicized form of this word is *architect*. We know that in construction, the only person whose word counts is the architect's. This was Paul's position. No one else's word counts; only Paul's word counts because he had the blueprint.

We see the same thing at the time of Moses. Moses received the pattern of the tabernacle from God, and he supervised the building work. Moses was the one who had the dimensions of the tabernacle and the ways to construct it with all the utensils. In the building of the tabernacle, only his word counted; no one else's word counted. If everyone would have had his say in that work, I am afraid there would have been a hundred or two hundred different kinds of tabernacles. This is

the situation with Christianity today. There are thousands
of churches. Every one of them is different, and every one of
them wants to build up its own group. The Anglican Church
builds up its own church. The Presbyterian Church builds up
its own church. The Catholic Church builds up its own church,
and the charismatics build up their own tongue-speaking
churches. Where is there a church that is built according to
the proper pattern? There is none. No one is building according to the blueprint that Paul received; no one is building
according to the revelation of the Bible. Everyone is building according to his own desire.

There is only one blueprint and one master builder in the
proper, correct building. The only master builder is the architect who has the blueprint in his hand. This is true in every
age. The Lord issues the blueprint, the revelation, and the
utterance, and through one man He supervises and completes
the building work. All those who do not build, speak, or serve
according to the blueprint released by the Lord through that
man are void of light and revelation and are not serving
according to the vision. Today in the Lord's recovery, some are
preaching and publishing messages. The portions in their
messages that impart light, revelation, and the life supply
invariably derive their source from this ministry in the Lord's
recovery. Other than those portions, there is no revelation or
vision in their writings.

Some have criticized us for not reading anything by out-
siders or the denominations. However, if there were any book
that contained light and revelation, why would those who
criticize us not take the lead to read it? Why would they be
reading the messages put out by this ministry instead? This
ministry produces nothing but gold and diamonds. You can
compare and see. For this reason, my dear brothers and sisters, today we are fighting the good fight for the truth. We
are bearing on our shoulders the commission of this age. This
is our vision. We have to be clear about this, and we have to
serve God according to this vision.

CHAPTER TWO

THE VISION OF A SERVING ONE

In the first chapter, entitled "Vision in God's Economy," we read how God's servants and the Lord's followers must see a vision. In this chapter we will continue with this burden by speaking about the vision of those who serve the Lord.

REVIEWING THE OLD TESTAMENT VISIONS

Adam's First Vision

According to the revelation of the entire Bible, the Lord began showing men a vision from the time of Adam. Before Adam fell, when he was first created, God showed him a clear yet relatively simple vision; he was placed in front of two trees in the garden of Eden and was told, "Of every tree of the garden thou mayest freely eat: but of the tree of the knowledge of good and evil, thou shalt not eat of it: for in the day that thou eatest thereof thou shalt surely die" (Gen. 2:16-17, KJV). This was the vision that God gave to Adam.

A vision is a scene that God unfolds to man. In the garden of Eden, when God gave Adam the command concerning the tree of life and the tree of the knowledge of good and evil, Adam saw a scene. That was the vision that God wanted to show him. That vision indicates something; it shows that God's intention is for man to eat the tree of life and to reject the tree of the knowledge of good and evil. For man to receive the tree of life means that he is living under this vision. It also means that he is serving God according to this vision. However, the devil, Satan, disguised as the serpent, seduced Eve through his speaking and turned her eyes from the tree of life to the tree of the knowledge of good and evil, against which God had warned her. Had Eve's vision been clear and had her heart closely followed the vision, she would have ignored the serpent when he spoke to her about the tree of the knowledge of good and evil and would not have talked about it or gazed upon it. Genesis 3:6 says, "And when the woman saw that the tree...." The minute Eve looked, she was distracted from the vision that God gave to man in the beginning.

The vision that God gave to Adam is the first vision in the entire Bible. The last vision is the New Jerusalem in the last two chapters of the book of Revelation. Between these two ends, God gave vision after vision to man.

Adam's Second Vision

After the first vision, Adam saw a second vision. After he and Eve fell, they knew that they were naked. As soon as they heard God's voice, they hid themselves among the trees of the garden to escape God's face. However, God did not give them up. Rather, He looked for them and gave them a vision. He said to the serpent, "And I will put enmity between thee and the woman, / and between thy seed and her seed; / it shall bruise thy head, / and thou shalt bruise his heel" (Gen. 3:15, KJV). This means that the seed of the woman would bruise the head of the serpent and would inflict upon him a death blow. The serpent, on the other hand, would bruise the heel of the seed of the woman and would frustrate His move. After this, God prepared a sacrifice—possibly a lamb—and made coats of skins to clothe Adam and Eve.

If we put all these acts of God together, we have a clear vision. It shows us that man is sinful and that there is an evil one who is trying to hurt him, but the seed of woman will come and will solve the problem of sin for him. He will bruise the head of the evil one. This vision also shows that man needs redemption; he needs the killing of the sacrifice and the shedding of the blood. He needs coats of skins to clothe him. This was the second vision that Adam saw. It is the second vision that God gave to man.

From that time onward, Adam began to live by this vision. He named his wife Eve (Gen. 3:20), which means "living." This indicates that he had heard and received the gospel. The judgment of death had passed over him, and he lived. Eve was also living by this vision, because when she bore a son, she called him Cain, which means "acquired." This indicates that in her concept, Cain was the acquired seed of the woman that God had promised. She believed in the seed and was waiting for the seed. We have to believe that Adam and Eve not only lived by the vision, but they also told their children about this vision.

Abel's Vision

According to the Scripture, the children of Adam were in two kinds of conditions. The first kind were those who lived under their fathers' vision, and the second were those who did not live under their fathers' vision; they took another way to serve and worship God. Abel belonged to the first kind; he lived under his father's vision, and his father's vision became his vision. Hence, he was serving God according to a vision. Cain belonged to the second kind. He did not take his father's vision, and he did not live by it. On the contrary, he invented another way of serving and worshipping God. He was absolutely not serving by a vision. By the second generation of mankind, it came to be that although all men were serving and worshipping the same true God, only Abel's service was carried out according to a vision. Cain was not worshipping idols; he did not serve other deities. Yet his service was one that was detached from the vision. He did not oppose God. On the contrary, he was also making sacrifices to God and worshipping God. Yet his sacrifice and worship were done apart from the vision; he was serving without a vision. This is the reason Abel was accepted by God while Cain was rejected by Him.

Enosh's Vision

The time of Enosh was the third generation of mankind. Here we see a further advance in vision. The fallen man discovered that he was a frail being, that he was nothing, could do nothing, and had nothing. He was as vain, frail, and empty as a puff of air. He needed reality, and reality is just God Himself. Hence, Enosh began to call on the name of Jehovah in hope of receiving reality from Him. In Exodus 3:15 God said to Moses, "Thus shalt thou say unto the children of

Israel, The Lord God of your fathers, the God of Abraham, the God of Isaac, and the God of Jacob, hath sent me unto you: this is my name for ever, and this is my memorial unto all generations" (KJV). This indicates that the name of Jehovah is the name of the Triune God. Therefore, for man to call on the name of Jehovah means to receive the Triune God into him to be his enjoyment and supply. For Enosh to call on the name of Jehovah means that he saw a greater vision. He realized that not only must the fallen man seek covering in God's righteousness through the shedding of the sacrificial blood, and not only must he trust in the coming One for the destruction of the enemy according to His revealed way, but this same fallen man must call on the name of Jehovah out of his vanity, nothingness, destitution, and impotence and live by the enjoyment of God's riches and supply. This indeed is a further advance in vision.

Enoch's Vision

Then came Enoch. He inherited Adam's vision, Abel's vision, and Enosh's vision, but he went on to see that he could not be separated from God. He needed to walk with God moment by moment. This is another vision. Enoch walked with God and did not see death (Heb. 11:5). He not only escaped the punishment of sin and the snare of transgressions, but was spared of death itself. In other words, by walking with God he was walking with the tree of life and was able to enjoy the tree of life because God is the very tree of life. Hence, we see a further progression of vision in the case of Enoch.

Noah's Vision

We have to believe that Noah at his time inherited Adam's vision, Abel's vision, Enosh's vision, and Enoch's vision. In addition, he received a further vision himself. In Genesis 6, God showed him clearly that the age was altogether evil. God wanted to give up and destroy that generation, and He wanted Noah to build an ark. Noah was living not only under the visions of Adam, Abel, Enosh, and Enoch; he was not only the heir of all these visions but was living, working, and serving under a greater vision which he saw with his own eyes. For this reason, we can say that Noah's life, work, and service were totally governed by the vision. We can believe that at the time of Noah, there were more than his family of eight people who were fearing God. Although the Bible does not say anything about this, we can deduce it from history. Surely there were other people who were worshipping God and serving Him. However, no matter how many people were worshipping God at that time, according to the record of the Bible, they were worshipping and serving apart from any vision. Only Noah and his family of eight were serving under a vision. This is very clear.

The Visions from Abraham to Joseph

At the time of Abraham, we see a more expansive and far-reaching vision. Abraham saw that one of his descendants would rise up and become a blessing to the nations. We can believe that Abraham did not drop the visions of Adam, Abel, Enosh, Enoch, and Noah. He inherited all these visions and was living under them. Yet he went on and saw a more expansive and far-reaching vision. After Abraham, we have Isaac. In Isaac we see a person who fully inherited Abraham's vision. Jacob was also an heir. After these three persons we have Joseph. In Joseph we have another vision. Through Egypt, the entire earth was blessed. Joseph was a type of Christ. He was a descendant of Abraham, yet he became the chief minister who managed all the food supply in Egypt. During the seven years of famine over the whole world, everyone came to Egypt and to Joseph for food. Hence, in Joseph we see a person through whom the entire earth was blessed. This is a picture of Christ ministering to and blessing the whole earth.

From Moses to David

Moses also saw a vision. He saw the tabernacle and the ordinances regarding the offerings and other matters, which we cannot describe here in detail. Joshua inherited from Moses and saw something further in the way of a vision. He led the Israelites into Canaan and inherited the good land.

During the time of the judges, there were visions after visions, until the time of Samuel. Samuel was also a man of vision, and he served according to the vision that he saw. Through him the age was changed from the confused age of the judges to the age of the kingdom. At the same time that Samuel was on earth, another person appeared on the scene—Saul. He was a king anointed by Samuel, yet he was not living by the vision. Another person who inherited from Samuel was David. He was a man living under the vision.

The Prophets

Beginning from the time of his reign, Solomon and his descendants gradually departed from all the visions. Nearly none of the kings during the age of the kings served according to a vision. Instead, they followed the custom of the nations. Under such circumstances God raised up the prophets. These prophets were not only living under a vision; they actually received visions. This is why the prophets were also called seers. Not only did they prophesy and speak for God; they saw vision after vision in a definite way and served according to these visions. At that time the kings had all departed from the visions that God had imparted to His people, so the prophets were raised up to correct and adjust them. They turned the kings back from the things contrary to the visions to a service that was once again under the visions. This is the story of the kings in the age of the kings.

The Conclusion of the Old Testament

The last two books of the Old Testament are Zechariah and Malachi. Both have certain rich utterances concerning Christ. They are the conclusion of the revelation concerning Christ in the Old Testament. There are three ways by which the Old Testament speaks about Christ—clear declarations, types, and prophecies. All these revelations concerning Christ come to a conclusion in the books of Zechariah and Malachi. They conclude everything. These two books speak much concerning Christ. This is the conclusion of the Old Testament.

THE VISIONS IN THE NEW TESTAMENT

The Vision of John the Baptist

At the time the Old Testament era ended, the earthly system of service was still in place. In Jerusalem of Judea there was still the temple, and there were still priests offering sacrifices, worshipping, and serving God according to the God-ordained institutions. Then suddenly John the Baptist appeared. He was not in the temple, and he was not a priest. He did not wear a priestly garment but instead lived in the wilderness, eating locusts and honey and wearing camel's hair. He was serving the Lord totally apart from the traditional rituals and ordinances. Please tell me who was serving according to a vision at that time: Was it the priests who were abiding by the traditions, or was it John the Baptist who had dropped all the traditions? The Gospel of John shows us clearly that the priests, the elders, the scribes, the Pharisees, and all the other Jewish religionists were serving God fully according to their religion, traditions, ordinances, knowledge, and doctrines. They were not under any vision. Only one man was serving under a vision—John the Baptist.

The Vision of the Lord Jesus and the Competition from John the Baptist

The ministry of John the Baptist was a kind of termination. It was for the purpose of ushering in a new beginning. The baptism of John the Baptist initiated the Lord Jesus into His office for the accomplishment of His ministry. John the Baptist clearly told us that his ministry was a pioneering and initiating ministry (John 1:23, 28-30), but his disciples did not understand this. They thought that John was a great man and that his teaching was unique. This was why they followed him and his teachings. Subconsciously, they began to compete with the Lord's ministry. Beginning from Matthew 9, we see the disciples of John questioning the Lord Jesus. Their questioning put them in the same category as the Pharisees (v. 14). According to Luke 5:33 it was the Pharisees who questioned Him, but Mark 2:18 seems to say that it was the disciples of John and the Pharisees together who questioned the Lord.

Before this time, the Pharisees were the only questioning party. After Matthew 9, John's disciples became another party.

At this point we see three parties: the Jewish religion, John's religion, and the Lord Jesus. All of them were serving God. Please tell me which of them were serving under a vision. No doubt those who followed the Lord Jesus were the only ones serving under a vision. Not only were the Jewish religionists not under the vision; even the Johannine religionists were not under the vision. God had set the Jewish religion aside and had used John the Baptist to bring in a new beginning, but when the Lord Jesus came, John's religion still remained on the scene competing with the Lord. God was forced by the situation to send John to prison. However, John still sent his disciples from his prison to the Lord Jesus to ask Him questions. On the one hand, the Lord commended John's ministry. On the other hand, He encouraged John to take the way that the Lord had ordained for him and to experience the blessing in that way. Soon after this, John was martyred. In this way God sovereignly ended the ministry of John.

Still, John's religion did not stop with his death. In Acts 18 and 19 this line reappeared and caused a problem. Apollos only knew the baptism of John, and he preached this when he went down to Ephesus (18:24-25; 19:3). This brought in the decline of the church. In the seven churches in Revelation 2 and 3, Ephesus shows us the beginning of the degradation of the church. John's religion was the source of this problem, and Apollos was the one who sowed the seed of this problem.

The Vision of the Followers of the Lord Jesus

While the Lord Jesus was fulfilling His ministry on the earth, those who were following Him were the only ones who had inherited the visions of the previous ages and who were at the same time catching up with the vision that matched that age. Not only had they inherited the visions that went before them, but they were caught up with the vision of that age when they followed the Lord Jesus. This group of people consisted of men like Peter, James, and John. None among the disciples were as foolish and uncouth as Peter. However, he was not foolish in one thing: While the Lord Jesus was shining on him as a great light and calling him by the Sea of Galilee, he together with Andrew, James, and John responded to the light and was attracted by the Lord to drop everything to follow Him (Matt. 4:15-16, 18-22). Andrew was first a disciple of John the Baptist (John 1:35-40). Now he and Peter, James, and John forsook the Jewish religion and John's religion. They even forsook their fishing career, leaving behind their fathers and their nets, and followed the Lord single-heartedly.

Outwardly speaking, Peter was following blindly. He was blindly following for three and a half years. Every day he was speaking nonsense. However, once, and only once, he spoke a clear word. When the Lord took the disciples up to the region of Caesarea Philippi and asked them who the Son of Man was, Peter answered, "You are the Christ, the Son of the living God" (Matt. 16:16). This was a word full of revelation. Unfortunately he only spoke one clear word. After this, he spoke many foolish words again. When the Lord indicated to the disciples that He had to go to Jerusalem to suffer under the hands of the elders, the chief priests, and the scribes and would be killed and then resurrected after three days, Peter took Him aside and rebuked Him, saying, "God be merciful to You, Lord! This shall by no means happen to You!" (vv. 21-22). But the Lord turned and said to Peter, "Get behind Me, Satan!" (v. 23). This shows us that Peter was indeed following blindly. He did not know what he was doing. He followed blindly but rightly. Sometimes when a person is too clear, he ends up doing the wrong thing. When he is a little foolish, he lands in the right place. At that time all those who were following the Lord Jesus, male or female, including such ones as Mary, were all foolish. Today we may appear foolish, but we can follow the Lord faithfully.

From the Bible we can see that not too many who followed the Lord were clear. Even the Lord Jesus' own mother, Mary, was not so clear. She was also somewhat muddled. She spoke some foolish words a few times and was rebuked. Although they were all foolish, they were foolish in the right direction. Men like Nicodemus who were so "clear" were not doing better in any way. Although they were clear that the Lord had the vision, they were not absolute in following Him. They were only following Him in a halfhearted way. Actually, they were only trailing behind Him and not following Him. I believe that among those who were "following" the Lord, Nicodemus was the clearest one and Peter the most foolish one. Yet the one who was the most foolish was the one who followed in the most genuine way. Although sometimes he failed, he was the most absolute one in following. When the Lord told the disciples that they would all be stumbled because of Him, Peter responded by saying, "If all will be stumbled because of You, I will never be stumbled." The Lord told him, "Truly I say to you that in this night, before a rooster crows, you will deny Me three times." Peter then said, "Even if I must die with You, I will by no means deny You" (Matt. 26:31-35). Of course, he did not keep his promise. On the contrary, he denied the Lord three times as was foretold by Him. Although he was such a person, he took the right path, and he followed the vision.

Peter's Vision

The One whom the disciples followed all the time eventually brought them to the cross. They were crucified with Him, died with Him, were buried with Him, and resurrected and ascended with Him (Eph. 2:6). On the day of Pentecost, Peter saw the vision. Formerly, he only identified himself with the vision through the Lord Jesus. Now at Pentecost, he saw the vision himself. When he stood up to speak, he was no longer foolish. He was very strong and clear in everything. In Acts 2 through 5, we find him caring for nothing other than the Lord's ministry. He did not even care for his own life. The vision did not find any resistance or hindrance in him at all.

When we come to Acts 10, however, we find that his strong Jewish background stood in the way and caused the vision to suffer a setback. In Matthew 16 the Lord told Peter that He would give him the keys to the kingdom. The *keys* are plural in number, indicating that there are at least two keys. On the day of Pentecost, Peter used one key to open the door for the Jews to enter God's New Testament kingdom. At that time the vision did not suffer any setback in him. However, by the time God wanted to use him further to exercise the second key to open the door to the Gentiles and to spread His New Testament economy among the Gentiles, Peter was lagging behind. This became a problem to God; He was forced to revert to the Old Testament means of visions and dreams. Peter saw a vessel like a great sheet descending from heaven to the earth. In it were all the four-footed animals and reptiles of the earth and birds of heaven. A voice came to him: "Rise up, Peter; slay and eat! But Peter said, By no means, Lord, for I have never eaten anything common and unclean. And a voice came to him again a second time: The things that God has cleansed, do not make common" (vv. 13-15). This went on three times. By this we can see that Peter had a problem in following the vision.

If we study Acts 10, Galatians 2, and Acts 15, we will find that, in those cases, Peter was no longer as absolute and strong in following the vision as he was in following the Lord during the first three and a half years. He became somewhat weak. The vision had come into conflict with his tradition, and he could not quite go along with it. He remained to a certain extent in that tradition. It frustrated him and hindered him from going on. We see a falling behind in his case with respect to the vision. We have to pay attention to this matter and be warned by it.

Paul's Vision

By the time of Acts 13, another person appeared on the scene. In Acts 7—9 he was Saul of Tarsus, a person who was in the Jewish religion and had received the highest education. He had also studied the best Greek culture and was an endeavoring man. At that time Judaism was under attack. The followers of Jesus Christ, the so-called "Nazarenes" (24:5), were getting stronger and stronger. Saul could not suffer to see his ancestors' religion being destroyed, and he became very zealous, being determined to wipe out the Nazarenes and to uphold his fathers' religion.

We cannot deny that Saul of Tarsus was serving God. After he was saved, he told the believers, "For you have heard of my manner of life formerly in Judaism, that I persecuted the church of God excessively and ravaged it. And I advanced in Judaism beyond many contemporaries in my race, being more abundantly a zealot for the traditions of my fathers" (Gal. 1:13-14). As to zeal, he was a persecutor of the church (Phil. 3:6). He was so zealous that he consented to Stephen's death (Acts 7:60—8:1a). He also put many believers into prison, cast votes to condemn them to death, and persecuted them even as far as foreign cities (26:9-11). Saul was indeed serving God, but he was serving without a vision. While he was being zealous for his fathers' traditions, who was serving God under a vision? It was Peter. Peter was under a vision, and those who were following him were also under the same vision. Saul, however, was not under the vision, yet one day on his way to Damascus the Lord met him and showed him the vision.

I truly believe that the vision Saul saw on the way to Damascus was more advanced than the one Peter saw. In the New Testament records concerning Peter and in his own Epistles, we do not see any mention of the Triune God working Himself into us to make us His duplication. We do not see anything about the believers being built up into the Body of Christ to be one with the Triune God as His organism. But on the way to Damascus, Paul saw a vision. The Lord said to him, "Saul, Saul, why are you persecuting Me?" (Acts 9:4). The *Me* here is a corporate *Me;* it includes the Lord Jesus and all His believers. Although the word *Me* is a small word, it speaks of a great vision. Paul in Galatians 1 says that "it pleased God...to reveal His Son in me" (vv. 15-16). In the Bible we do not find that Peter saw the same clear vision.

Paul's vision was indeed profound. At the beginning of Galatians, he refers to the Son of God (1:16). When we speak of the Son of God, we have to realize that this involves the Triune God. The Triune God was revealed to Paul, and Paul became one of His members. All the members together with Paul were constituted to become His Body and were joined to Him to become an enlarged "Me." Although the vision Paul saw at the beginning was so high and profound, he did not take up his ministry immediately. In Acts 13, a few prophets and teachers were serving the Lord and fasting together in

Antioch. It was then that the Holy Spirit said, "Set apart for Me now Barnabas and Saul for the work to which I have called them" (v. 2). It was not until then that Paul became clear about the vision he had received earlier and was sent to fulfill the ministry which he had received.

Both Barnabas and Saul were Jews, yet they were sent to preach the gospel throughout the Gentile lands. This was not a small vision. In his own time, Peter was only sent to make a brief contact with a Gentile and to visit his home. Here Paul received a serious commission: "Go, for I will send you forth far away to the Gentiles" (22:21). This means he was to go to the Gentile lands nation by nation and city by city. This is a great vision: "That in Christ Jesus the Gentiles are fellow heirs and fellow members of the Body and fellow partakers of the promise through the gospel" (Eph. 3:6).

Many of us have been affected by Christianity; we read the Bible in a superficial way. We think that Paul was sent to merely preach the gospel and to save sinners from hell. In reading the book of Acts, many believers come away with the impression that the Lord's desire is to spread the gospel to the uttermost part of the earth. They see the great number of sinners in the Gentile world and consider that they cannot be saved unless the believers go out to preach the gospel to them. To them this was why Paul was sent on his evangelistic journey to preach the gospel. However, if we carefully study the book of Acts and Paul's Epistles, we will discover that this matter is not that simple or shallow. Paul was sent to preach to the Gentiles the unsearchable riches of Christ (Eph. 3:8) in order that the Triune God could be dispensed into them to transform them into the members of Christ for the building up of the Body of Christ. At this time, Paul's vision became fully clear.

Factors of Frustrations

The Problem of Judaism

Here we have to ask, while Paul was fulfilling his ministry, who on earth was clear about God's vision? At that time there were still many God-fearing people in the Jewish religion.

For example, Gamaliel feared God; he understood the Old Testament and was familiar with the teachings of the Old Testament, yet he was not in Paul's vision.

The Problem of the Church in Jerusalem

At that time Peter and John were in Jerusalem. There was also a very pious James. These were the leading ones in the church in Jerusalem (Gal. 2:9). At the time Paul was fulfilling his ministry, it seems that James and Peter were one with his vision. However, they were not one with it. The best we can say about them is that they did not oppose Paul. They were going along in a general way but were actually not in the same company. They received the same grace as Paul did, and they were apostles together. They should have belonged to the same group and the same company. Yet they were not of the same company, though they were of the same general group. Galatians 2:9 says that James, Peter, and John gave to Paul and Barnabas the right hand of fellowship that they should go to the Gentiles, while they would go to the circumcision. It seems as if they were shaking hands with Paul and saying to him, "Okay, Paul. Go to the Gentiles to fulfill your ministry, but we will not go with you. We are here to be apostles to the Jews, while you go to be the apostle to the Gentiles."

The Problem of Barnabas

I do not believe too many Christians have detected this flavor when they read the Bible. Faced with this situation, Paul surely must not have had a sweet feeling. Fortunately Barnabas was with him, but not long after this, the two had an argument. In the end Barnabas left. This shows that even Barnabas could not catch up with the vision of that age, the vision which Paul saw. Although he was the one who ushered Paul into the service, when Paul saw the up-to-date vision of the age, Barnabas was left behind.

The Problem of James

Not only were men like Gamaliel and Barnabas falling behind in the vision; even apostles such as Peter and James were in danger of missing out on the vision. They were of the same general group as Paul, but they were not co-working together. When Paul went up to Jerusalem for the last time, James said to him, "You observe, brother, how many thousands there are among the Jews who have believed; and all are zealous for the law" (Acts 21:20). Before this time, Paul had said clearly in Galatians that the law is over. But here, James, the leading apostle in Jerusalem, was exhorting him to keep the law. This shows us that even a person as renowned in the church as James could be short in the vision. James did not walk according to the flesh; he was not a light person in any way. From history we know that he was quite a pious person. Yet he was not serving under the vision. We can say that even Peter did not catch up with the vision; even he was not in the vision.

The record of the Jerusalem conference in Acts 15 shows us that this decision was full of Judaistic influence. James's word was saturated with a Jewish and Old Testament overtone. I do not believe that decision could have satisfied Paul. Yet in order to keep the peace, he tolerated the decision, for without such a decision, there would have been unceasing arguments between the Jewish and Gentile churches over the matter of circumcision, and the churches would forever be in turmoil. However, things did not turn out as he had hoped. That decision did not solve in a clear and accurate way the problem of the Old Testament law. This proves that the church in Jerusalem did not come up fully to the vision of the age; instead, it made a compromise.

The Problem of Apollos

In Acts 18, Apollos appeared on the scene. He was "powerful in the Scriptures" (v. 24b). We have to realize that the Scriptures here refer to the thirty-nine books of the Old Testament. Apollos was powerful in expounding the Old Testament, but he was not in Paul's vision. At that time, Aquila, Priscilla, and Timothy joined Paul's ministry one after another. No doubt they were in Paul's vision. They were walking with Paul and working together with him.

Paul worked throughout the Gentile world, but he never stayed in one place for as long as three years except in Ephesus. Acts 20:31 tells us clearly that Paul stayed in Ephesus for three years. His preaching affected the entire region of Asia, of which Ephesus was the center. Paul was teaching there, and his teaching affected all those who were in Asia, but at the same time in Ephesus a negative seed was sown, and Apollos was the one who sowed it. This is one of the reasons why Paul had to work and minister in Ephesus for three years. In Acts 20, after Paul finished traveling to all the places to exhort the believers, he passed by Ephesus, called the elders together, and charged them, saying, "Take heed to yourselves and to all the flock....I know that after my departure fierce wolves will come in among you, not sparing the flock" (vv. 28-29).

After this Paul went up to Jerusalem, and soon he was bound and sent to prison. He was imprisoned in Caesarea for two years (Acts 24:27), after which he was sent to Rome. In Rome he was imprisoned for at least another two years (28:30). After he was released from prison, he wrote the first Epistle to Timothy, in which he began by saying, "Even as I exhorted you, when I was going into Macedonia, to remain in Ephesus in order that you might charge certain ones not to teach different things" (1:3). This word shows us a trace of some kind of problem in Ephesus. A little over a year after Paul was released from prison, Nero, the Roman emperor, began to persecute the church again, and Paul was sent back to prison. While he was in prison, he wrote the second Epistle to Timothy. In 1:15 he said, "All who are in Asia turned away from me." Among these churches who had turned away from Paul, Ephesus was the leading one. Hence, in Revelation, the first of the seven letters to the seven churches was to the church in Ephesus.

The seed that Apollos sowed in Ephesus eventually became the basic factor for the decline of the church. The reason that the church in Ephesus degraded was that it had taken the lead to depart from the teaching of the apostles. To depart from the apostles' teaching is to depart from the apostles' vision. With the departure of the apostles' teaching came

the teaching of Balaam (Rev. 2:14), the teaching of the Nicolaitans (vv. 6, 15), and the teaching of Jezebel (v. 20). These
three teachings represent all the heresies in Christianity.
Paul tells us in Colossians that the ministry he received
from God was to complete the word of God (1:25). After Paul
completed his ministry and finished his Epistles, the church
in Ephesus took the lead to bring all the churches in Asia
away from the teaching of the apostle Paul. By the time the
book of Revelation was written, we find the apostle John con-
tinuing the Lord's commission and following Paul in fulfilling
his ministry. John continued from where Paul had left off in
his ministry. While Paul was on earth, he dealt with the problem of decline. The last church he dealt with was Ephesus in
Asia. Thirty years later, at the beginning of the book of Revelation, in writing to the seven churches in Asia, the first
church that was addressed was the church in Ephesus. John
rebuked Ephesus for having left its first love. The reason it
had left its first love is that it had left the apostles' teaching.

The Vision of the Apostle John—
the Ultimate Consummation of God's Visions

The book of Revelation, which the apostle John wrote,
begins with the seven churches. It covers this age and extends
to the coming of Christ, the judgment of the world, and the
advent of the millennium, and it concludes with the New
Jerusalem in the new heaven and new earth. This constitutes
the ultimate consummation of the divine revelation. After this
there is nothing more left to be said or seen. Everything is said
and everything is seen. This is the ultimate consummation of
God's economy. Once the New Jerusalem appears, we have the
final scene. This is why the end of Revelation says that nothing can be added to or deleted from this book (22:18-19). From
that time onward, no one could add anything to the Bible. If
anyone tries to add anything, his portion will be the punishment of the lake of fire. No one can delete anything. If anyone
tries to cut off anything, he will be cut off from the blessing of
the tree of life, the water of life, and the city of life. This shows
us that at the end of Revelation, God's vision is consummated.

No one can see more, and those who see less will, of course, suffer loss.

SERVING GOD ACCORDING TO THE COMPLETE VISION

From the time the apostle John completed the book of Revelation until today, nineteen centuries have passed. During the past nineteen hundred years, countless numbers of Christians have been serving God. Added to this great number of Christians serving God are the Jews, who also are serving God. Of course, the Jews serve only according to the vision of the Old Testament. Some Christians are serving according to the vision revealed in the New Testament Gospels, which has to do only with the earthly ministry of Jesus. Some serve without any vision at all. In order to serve God according to the up-to-date vision, we have to come up to the level of Paul's very last Epistles. In fact, we have to come up to the level of the epistles to the seven churches in Revelation as well as the revelation which covers all the ages, including the kingdom, the new heaven and new earth, and the ultimate consummation of the church—the New Jerusalem. Simply put, in order for us to serve God today, our vision must extend all the way from the first vision of Adam in Genesis to the ultimate vision of the manifestation of the church, the New Jerusalem. This and this alone is the complete vision. It is not until today that this vision has been fully opened to us.

In the National Palace Museum in Taipei, there is a painting on a long scroll called "The River Scene at Ching-Ming Festival." It describes in detail the culture, life, and way of the Chinese people at the time of the painting. It is not enough to see only the first few portions of that long scroll. One has to go all the way from one end to the other end before he can have a clear picture, or "vision," of the entire spectrum of life in China. In the same way, we have our own painting, our "River Scene at Ching-Ming," in our service to God. It begins from Adam's vision of the tree of life in the garden of Eden and extends all the way to the New Jerusalem with the tree of life. The New Jerusalem is the last scene of the vision. After that there is nothing more to be seen.

The problem today is, who has seen this complete vision,

and who is living in this vision? During the past nineteen hundred years, many people have been serving the Lord, but how have they served? Can we say that five hundred years ago Martin Luther saw this vision and was serving according to this vision? Throughout the ages many people were serving the Lord only according to the first few scenes. I wish that all the brothers and sisters would have an enlarged and far-reaching view. I hope they will realize that all the books that we have put out cover the entire spectrum from the first scene to the last scene. We are not serving God based on the first few scenes alone. We are serving God according to the last scene which includes all the previous scenes.

Today many people have not seen what we have seen. They are merely serving according to the first few scenes, and they are even arguing with one another. The Jews are pious people; they are zealous in expounding the Scriptures from Genesis to Malachi, but they have only the Old Testament. Many Christians love the Lord and are zealous for the gospel. Yet they preach only the story of Jesus Christ. They have never progressed beyond the four Gospels. Some have seen only the vision of the book of Acts. Others have seen the vision of the Epistles. All these are fragmentary, but we should serve God according to the entire spectrum, from the first scene of Adam to the last scene in Revelation. This is why we face so much opposition. Many people say that we are wrong. They criticize us for "stealing sheep." It is not that they do not love the Lord or serve God; it is that they love the Lord and serve God only according to the vision which they themselves have seen. Today we must be clear about the standing that we take. The goal of all our services, including preaching the gospel and edifying the believers, must be ultimately consummated in the New Jerusalem. Only then will we be unshaken in the face of any criticism.

CLOSELY FOLLOWING
THE COMPLETED VISION OF THIS AGE

Since we have the up-to-date and ultimate vision, we should closely follow after it. We are absolutely not following a man; rather, we are following a vision. It is grossly wrong to say that we are following a certain person. We are following a vision that belongs to the present age. It is God's consummate vision.

The Lord's recovery was brought to us through our dear Brother Nee. Because of this he became a target of attack. In 1934 he was married in Hangchow. Some took this opportunity to stir up a storm. He became very sad, so one day I went to him to comfort him, saying, "Brother Nee, you know that between the two of us, there is no natural relationship. I do not take the way that you are taking or preach what you are preaching out of a natural friendship with you. The two of us are widely separated from one another. I am a northerner and you are a southerner. Today I am taking the same pathway not because I am following you as a person. I am following the way that you are taking. Brother Nee, I would like you to know that even if one day you do not take this way, I will still take this way." I said this because the storm affected some, and they decided not to take this way anymore. In other words, many people were following a man. When the man seemed to have changed, they turned away. But I told Brother Nee, "Even if one day you do not take this way, I will still take this way. I am not taking this way because of you, and I will not leave this way because of you. I have seen that this is the Lord's way. I have seen the vision."

Fifty-two years have passed. Today I do not regret at all what I have done. During the past fifty-two years, I have seen the same story repeat itself again and again. Some people came and left. One scene changed and another scene came along. Since the beginning of our work in Taiwan, during the past three decades, we have witnessed some major crises. Even brothers whom I led to salvation and who went through my very own training left the Lord's recovery. The vision has never changed, but the persons have indeed changed, and those who follow the vision also have changed. I would say a sober word to all of you from the bottom of my heart. By the Lord's mercy, I can stand here today to bring you this vision. I hope that you are not following me as a person; I hope that by the Lord's mercy you are following the vision that I have shown you.

I have no intention to be proud. America is the leading country in this world. It is also the top Christian country. There are many theological professors there. When I went there, I spoke boldly about the vision that I saw. At the beginning their ears were pricked, but by now, some are speaking what we have seen. Up until today, they are not able to put out a proper book to refute the truth that I have released. In order for them to write a book to refute me, they must first read my books, but once they read my books, they are convinced and subdued. They cannot refute anymore. Rather, they have to admit, "If you carefully and seriously read what this old Chinese man has written, you will discover that he has a solid basis for what he is saying. It is best not to challenge him in any matter. If you do, he can come back and ask you ten questions, none of which you can answer." They are very clear about this.

I would like to relate to you one fact. It is the Lord's mercy that He has revealed to me the vision. I advise you not to follow me, but to follow this vision which Brother Nee and all the servants of the Lord throughout the ages have left to us, which I have handed to you. This is indeed the vision that extends from the first scene of Adam to the last scene of the New Jerusalem. Over fifty years have passed. I have seen with my own eyes that those who take the way of the Lord's recovery for a while and then leave do not come to a proper ending. There is only one way. All spiritual things are one. There is one God, one Lord, one Spirit, one church, one Body, one testimony, one way, one flow, and one work. If you do not take this way, you will have no way to take.

Some who left us once shouted and boldly declared that they had seen the vision. Today where is their vision? After so much shouting, the vision is lost. They have lost the way. To start a war one must have the proper cause. With a proper cause we have the boldness to say what we say. If we do not take this way today, what other way do we have? I speak this for myself also. What other cause can we take up? Between 1942 and 1948 there was a greater storm, and Brother Nee was forced to discontinue his ministry for six years. At that time some saints who appreciated Brother Nee very much said, "Let us start another meeting." Brother Nee said, "You must never do this. The church is the church; if it agrees with me, it is the church. If it does not agree with me, it is still the church. We can never set up another meeting apart from the church."

Paul told Timothy, "All who are in Asia turned away from me" (2 Tim. 1:15), but Paul did not authorize Timothy to have another start. In the same way, at the time when almost everyone in China forsook Brother Nee, he did not try to make another start. This proves that even Paul and Brother Nee could not change the way they took. If they were to change the way, they would not have been able to go on.

This is my burden. I hope that you will clearly see the vision of the Lord's recovery and will follow this vision. You are not following me as a person. Sister Faith Chang can testify for me. She witnessed how I followed Brother Nee absolutely, yet I was not following the person; I was following the vision that he saw. In that age, the vision that came up to God's standard was the vision that Brother Nee saw. If you remained in that vision, you were serving according to the vision. If you did not remain in that vision, you were not serving according to the vision. Today Brother Nee has passed away. I have no intention to make a new start, but the Lord has commissioned me with this ministry. I can only take the lead willingly and obediently. The vision that I have brought to you today is God's vision for this age. If you remain in this vision, you are serving according to the vision. If you do not remain in this vision, you should be aware of what your end will be.

Therefore, you are not following a man; rather, you are standing with the Lord's ministry. You are following a vision, a vision that matches the age, a vision that inherits all that was in the past and a vision that is all-inclusive. It is up-to-date, and yet it builds on the past. If you remain in the book of Acts, you may have inherited everything prior to that time, but you are not up-to-date. Today as we stand here and ponder the revelations unveiled in the Lord's recovery, as we read the publications that are released among us, we can see that they cover everything from the church to God's economy to the New Jerusalem in the new heaven and new earth. This is a bountiful and all-sufficient vision. If you remain in this vision, you are serving according to the vision. If you are not in this vision, you could still be an Apollos, expounding the Scriptures in a powerful way; you could still be a Barnabas, visiting the churches; you could still be a James, serving piously; and you could even be a Peter, who served as the leading apostle. However, you would not be in the vision. I believe this light is very clear among us. No one can argue with this. I hope that the young brothers and sisters will all be clear about this. From your youth, while you are serving the Lord, you should understand what we are doing here. This is not a personal thing. It is absolutely the Lord's ministry. He has unveiled the visions generation after generation to His children. All those who are in this vision now are serving according to God's vision.

THE GENUINE ONE ACCORD

Where there is no vision, the people cast off restraint, because there is no one accord. It is true that many people love the Lord and serve God, but everyone has his opinion and his own vision. As a result, there is no way to have the one accord. This is why Christianity has become so weak. God's people are divided and split apart. There are divisions everywhere. Although everyone says that he loves the Lord, there is no clear vision, and men are "carried about by every wind." Some among us also doubt, saying, "Are we the only ones who are right? Do not others also preach the gospel? Do they not also bring men to the Lord and edify them? Consider the aged James. He was more pious than Paul or Brother Nee. How can we say that he did not have a vision?"

Recently while we were translating the New Testament Recovery Version, I used two Catholic translations among my references. In some expressions we felt that these Catholic translations are not bad. I joked with my helpers, saying, "In this sentence, let us follow the Catholic Church." My point is this: Although James was pious to the uttermost in Jerusalem, we cannot conclude from this that his pathway was the right one. We cannot conclude from this that he possessed the vision that matched the age. No, we must be clear what the genuine vision is.

I believe this word will answer many questions in your heart. Although we are far behind many people in their zeal for preaching the gospel, although many people are more zealous and more burning in spirit than we are, and although we are poor, the vision is still with us. I truly hope that the young workers among us and the trainees would exercise themselves unto godliness. It does not mean that once we have the vision we do not need to have godliness anymore, yet I hope that you would remember that godliness alone cannot match the vision. Indeed, we need to exercise ourselves unto godliness; we should not be loose, and our personality and character should be noble. But this does not mean that once we have a noble character we are in the vision. In other words, our vision should be one that matches the age. It should also be one that includes everything that has gone before us. It should include the godliness of the Jews, the zeal of the evangelicals, and the genuine service. Only then will we be able to practice an all-inclusive church life, the church life Paul revealed to us (Rom. 14). We are not divided into sects, and we do not impose any special practice on anyone. We only live an all-inclusive church life. If we do this, we will have the genuine one accord.

Today we can be in one accord because we have only one vision and one view. We are all in this up-to-date, all-inheriting vision. We have only one viewpoint. We speak the same thing with one heart, one mouth, one voice, and one tone, serving the Lord together. The result is a power that will become our strong morale and our impact. This is our strength. Once the Lord's recovery possesses this power, there will be the glory of increase and multiplication. Today our situation is not yet to that point; it is not yet at the peak. Although we do not have many major contentions, we do have some small complaints and criticisms. These things lower our morale.

When I returned to Taiwan in 1984, there was no morale at all. Why? It is because the one accord was gone. The goal was gone and the vision became blurred. At this time we hope that the Lord would be merciful to us. We want to recover our morale, beginning from Taiwan. We want to recover our vision. We want to have the one accord, and we want to see clearly that there is only this one way. The churches in the Lord's recovery should have the Lord's testimony and a definite standing. Today there is still much ground for us to cover in the spreading of the Lord's churches. We have to preach the gospel everywhere, build up the small groups, and teach the truth. With this goal in view, we should have no arguments and no different opinions. We should speak the same thing, think the same thing, and press on in one accord. Not only should the churches in Taiwan do this, but all the churches in all the continents throughout the earth should do this. If we do this, the power will be great. The Lord will surely grant us an open door because this is the way that the Lord wants to take today.

CHAPTER THREE

THE PRESENT VISION AND PRACTICE IN THE LORD'S RECOVERY

Paul writes in 1 Timothy 1:3, "Even as I exhorted you, when I was going into Macedonia, to remain in Ephesus in order that you might charge certain ones not to teach different things." This verse shows that Paul was inwardly clear that there were some in Ephesus who were teaching differently. For this reason, he charged one of his closest co-workers, Timothy, to remain in Ephesus to help the Ephesian believers and even charge them not to teach different doctrines or teachings. This proves that the matter of different teachings is a serious matter.

THE HEALTHY TEACHING

In 6:3 Paul writes again, "If anyone teaches different things and does not consent to healthy words, those of our Lord Jesus Christ, and the teaching which is according to godliness." This is one of Paul's final words in this book, which reminds us of his opening word. What is it to teach differently? It is to not consent to healthy words. These healthy words are the words of our Lord Jesus Christ. We have to realize that those who were teaching differently were teaching the words of the Old Testament. Although the Old Testament words are part of the Scriptures, they are not the "healthy words." *Unhealthy words* here means words that do not minister or supply life to others. What then are the "healthy words"? They are the words of the Lord Jesus in the New Testament age and the teaching that is according to godliness.

First Timothy 3:15-16 says, "The house of God, which is the church of the living God, the pillar and base of the truth.

And confessedly, great is the mystery of godliness: He who was manifested in the flesh...." If we put all the above verses together we can see that the healthy teaching includes two parts. The first part is the words that the Lord Jesus Himself spoke. The other part is the words that the apostles spoke on earth after the Lord resurrected and ascended. These words are "the teaching which is according to godliness." The teaching which is according to godliness concerns God becoming flesh, passing through human living, dying, and resurrecting to produce the church, which is God manifested in the flesh. What the church supports and upholds is the teaching according to godliness, which is God manifesting Himself in the flesh through the church. In reality, the healthy teaching covers the entire New Testament; it is constituted with the Lord Jesus' words of life and the preaching of the apostles, which is the word of the mystery of godliness, that is, of God becoming flesh to produce the church. It extends all the way from Matthew to Revelation.

Paul's burden in his first Epistle to Timothy was to instruct him to remain in Ephesus to charge the dissenters not to teach anything outside the New Testament teaching. If anyone teaches anything apart from the New Testament teaching, he is teaching differently, and he does not consent to healthy words. If we study this book carefully, we will see that at that time there were some Judaistic Christians who were spreading such things as Old Testament knowledge and genealogies, not only among Jewish believers in Jerusalem but among the churches in all the Gentile lands. Although their speaking was in accordance with the Old Testament, it was not the healthy words. Consider the case of circumcision. According to the record of Genesis 17, God established circumcision with Abraham as a sign of an eternally immutable covenant. The Jewish Christians argued that even in the New Testament age, God's people, that is, His children, were not exempt from circumcision. Superficially, such a teaching sounds scriptural. Actually, it is absolutely contrary to God's New Testament economy which the apostles preached.

Moreover, these preachings which were superficially scriptural did not give life to men. They did not afford men any life supply. On the contrary, they led some to become shipwrecked regarding the faith (1 Tim. 1:19). Therefore, they were unhealthy teachings. Healthy words are those that are not only scriptural, but those that consent to the revelation of the Lord Jesus. They cover the speakings concerning His birth, death, and resurrection. They also cover the words which the apostles continued to speak after His ascension concerning God becoming flesh and passing through death and resurrection to release God's life and to produce the church to be the corporate manifestation of God in the flesh. These words according to the mystery of godliness are the consistent and overall revelation of God in the New Testament.

THE BACKGROUND
OF THE FIRST EPISTLE TO TIMOTHY

In order to understand 1 Timothy, we must first understand the background behind the writing of this book. In Acts 20, we find Paul sending for the elders of the church in Ephesus while he was on his way to Jerusalem. He spoke a solemn and crucial word to them. He reminded them how for three years he was in their midst, not shrinking from declaring to them all the counsel of God (vv. 20, 27, 31). This means that Paul fully and thoroughly explained to them God's revelation in the New Testament. Then he said, "I know that after my departure fierce wolves will come in among you, not sparing the flock" (v. 29). The wolves here refer to the Judaistic believers. They were doing an unhealthy work in the church, speaking unhealthy words. Unhealthy words are poisonous words, killing words. Those who were speaking these unhealthy words destroyed men and poisoned them rather than supplied them. In this sense, they were like wolves. In John 10 the Lord said that He is the good Shepherd and that He came to lay down His life that men may receive life (vv. 10-11). He also said that the wolf comes not to give life but to snatch and scatter (v. 12). Hence, everyone who causes harm and destruction in the church is a wolf. Outwardly, those who teach differently are God's people, but the different teaching that they are teaching is the unhealthy teaching. To be unhealthy means to not supply men with life. This is to harm and destroy. This may be compared to

the food that we eat: if it is not healthy, it is harmful. If we eat
unhealthy food, not only will it not benefit us, but it will actually harm our body and threaten our physical life.

Paul's Burden

The Bible is written like a jigsaw puzzle. It is not written in
a systematic way. Rather, it says a little here and a little there.
We have to spend the time to put all the pieces together. In
Acts 20, Paul knew that the church in Ephesus had a problem.
He was very concerned about the situation, and he sent for the
elders to come to him. He charged them repeatedly to be watch-
ful and sober and on the alert. After this, he left for Jerusalem.
Once he arrived in Jerusalem, problems arose. There the Christians were deeply into the practice of keeping the law. James
and the elders came to see Paul and said to him, "You observe,
brother, how many thousands there are among the Jews who
have believed; and all are zealous for the law" (21:20). Not only
were they keeping the law; they were even vowing the Nazarite
vow and purifying themselves (vv. 23b-24; Num. 6:2-5). This
indicates that the Jewish believers in Jerusalem were still
keeping the law of Moses and remaining in the Old Testament
age. Under the strong influence of Judaism, they mixed God's
New Testament economy with the out-of-date Old Testament
economy.

Being Entangled in James's Snare

However, James thought that this mixture was good. He
even told Paul, "And they have been informed concerning you
that you are teaching all the Jews throughout the nations apos-
tasy from Moses....What then is to be done? They will certainly
hear that you have come" (Acts 21:21-22). James was saying
that there were tens of thousands of believers in Jerusalem who
could not accept what Paul had done. As a result, Paul had an
evil name. What should he do? James advised him, saying,
"Therefore do this that we tell you: We have four men who have
a vow on themselves; take these and be purified with them, and
pay their expenses that they may shave their heads. And all
will know that there is nothing to the things that they have
been informed of concerning you, but that you yourself also

walk orderly, keeping the law" (vv. 23-24). The four had vowed a Nazarite vow. In order for a Nazarite to complete his vow, he had to pay a sum for the sacrifice (Num. 6:13-17). It was a substantial sum of money, so according to the Jewish tradition, those who paid on behalf of a poor Nazarite were not only considered pious but actually became partakers of the Nazarite vow.

Paul told us strongly in the books of Romans and Galatians that the law is over. Since that is the case, why would Paul have conceded to James's proposal when he was in Jerusalem and gone back to the law? Perhaps Paul was thinking, "Although I have written the books of Romans and Galatians, I have also written the book of 1 Corinthians. There I said that to the Jews I became as a Jew that I might gain the Jews (9:20). Since all the people here in Jerusalem are Jews, I can only be a Jew." To put it in a nice way, Paul did this in order to not be different from others. To put it in a not-so-nice way, Paul was compromising.

God's Sovereign Rescue for the Sake of His New Testament Economy

Although Paul tried to become as a Jew to the Jews and as a Gentile to the Gentiles, the Lord did not allow him to compromise. It was a serious thing for him to participate in that vow. It jeopardized God's New Testament economy to the uttermost. This was why after Paul stayed with the four men in the temple for six days, while waiting for the priests to come on the seventh day as the Nazarite vow was concluding, a riot suddenly broke out. Some Jews from Asia saw Paul in the temple, and they stirred up the crowd to seize him (Acts 21:27-30). Outwardly, it was the rioters who seized Paul. Actually, in God's eyes, it was a rescue to Paul.

I believe that while Paul stayed in the temple for nearly seven consecutive days, he was both ashamed and disgusted with the whole affair, yet he dared not express himself. He did not know what to do. It is very possible that he prayed desperately: "Lord, save me from this troubling situation. I have told others in the books of Romans and Galatians that Christ is the end of the law and that I have died to the law and have nothing to do with it anymore. I have said this so clearly. Even the ink of my writing may still be wet. How can I now go back to offer a sacrifice and keep the law? It is true that I have determined to become as a Jew among the Jews, but I will not remain in the Jewish land for long. I have to go to the Gentile lands to work. By then the news will have spread to these Gentile lands. The Gentile believers will ask me, 'Paul, what have you done? What happened to you? Your action did not match your word! We have been reading your Epistles. How are you going to explain to us what you have done? Why did you go back to Jerusalem to keep the ordinances of the law? How are you going to justify yourself?'" It is very possible that Paul prayed, "Lord, rescue me out of this troubling situation!" The Lord used the riot and rescued him in this way.

To the Jews, the reason for the riot was to kill Paul, but God in His sovereignty protected him. The news of the riot reached the commander of the cohort (v. 31). Immediately he brought soldiers to rescue Paul out of the hand of the Jews and keep him in custody. This was a big protection to Paul. It not only saved his life from the persecuting hands of the Jews, but it saved him from the peril of tearing down God's New Testament economy. In the end, Paul did not complete the Nazarite vow. This spared the church completely from the havoc of Judaism, but at the same time it also terminated the first part of Paul's ministry.

We already have covered this matter in detail in the *Life-study of Acts* (see messages 56 to 59). The events in Jerusalem eventually brought Paul to Caesarea. There he was kept for about two years. No doubt those two years were a very profitable and excellent time for Paul. They afforded him the peace to reconsider everything. In his prison he was separated from all the hindrances, distractions, frustrations, and influences. He surely would have realized that his going up to Jerusalem was a big mistake. Such pondering must have brought him under an open sky.

Actually, after the conference in Jerusalem in Acts 15, Paul's spirit was already quite troubled. He was not at peace about the situation in the church in Jerusalem. He must have been clear that the church in Jerusalem was in an ambiguous situation. It was not absolute for God's New Testament economy, and it contained a strong mixture of Old Testament elements. Jewish and Christian influences were all mixed up together. He could not have been at peace about it. Because his burden was so heavy, he was not able to forget about Jerusalem even during the third journey of his ministry. This must be why in 19:21 Paul purposed in his spirit to go to Jerusalem. I believe he had a strong desire to go to fellowship with James and to deal with the matter of the mixture. Little did he realize that not only would he not be able to fellowship much with James, but he would be forced into an embarrassing situation by James and the elders in Jerusalem. In the end he was subdued by James and fell into his trap.

However, God did not allow the situation to continue this way. His hand came in to intervene. First, He rescued Paul out of the mixture of the church in Jerusalem. At the same time, He rescued him out of the hands of the Jews who sought to kill him. In the end, Paul was kept in custody under the hands of the Romans and was isolated from the disturbance and riot. He remained in prison in Caesarea for two years. This afforded him a period of quiet reflection. It prepared him to write the last few Epistles, especially the Epistle to the Ephesians. Two years later, he appealed to Caesar. This brought him to Rome, where he remained in prison for another two years. During that period he wrote the Epistles to the Ephesians, Philippians, and Colossians. The thought in these three books is very deep. Such a thought had not been in him before he was put into prison. Neither had he ever written anything concerning it before this time. In these three books he unveiled God's economy, which concerns God's dispensing of Himself in His Divine Trinity into His chosen people in order that they may gain Christ, who is the Triune God Himself, for the producing of the members of Christ, being constituted as the organic Body of Christ to be the church of the living God to manifest Him.

Paul's Concern for the Church in Ephesus

From the time of Acts 20, Paul had been very concerned about the condition of the church in Ephesus. This was why he wrote to the church in Ephesus even while he was in prison, revealing to them God's economy, which is God's working Himself through His Divine Trinity into man, in order that man would enjoy the riches of Christ to become His members and be constituted into the Body of Christ for the manifestation of the Triune God. This is the central vision of God in the entire Bible. It is the consummating vision in both the Old and New Testaments. Later Paul was released from the Roman prison. He passed through Macedonia and wrote the first Epistle to Timothy, telling Timothy that some in Ephesus had a problem. He told Timothy to remain in Ephesus to charge them not to teach anything different from God's economy. This is the entire background of the writing of the first Epistle to Timothy.

THE BACKGROUND
OF THE SECOND EPISTLE TO TIMOTHY

A little over a year after Paul was released from prison, Nero, the Roman Caesar, began to persecute the Christians. He put leaders such as Peter and Paul into prison. After Paul went into prison again, he wrote the second Epistle to Timothy. Before his second imprisonment, there were many Jews among the churches in the Gentile lands who were beginning to teach Old Testament things different from the New Testament teaching. By the time Paul went into prison, the Judaizing Christians had become even more aggressive. Perhaps they told others, "See? Paul is in prison. If his teachings were right, why would God have allowed him to end up in prison?" Paul's imprisonment gave the Judaizing Christians and those who taught differently a strong ground to speak. This is the reason Paul wrote the second Epistle to Timothy.

The two Epistles to Timothy were written about two years apart. Therefore, Timothy did not remain in Ephesus for a long time. In 2 Timothy 1:13 Paul said, "Hold a pattern of the healthy words that you have heard from me, in the faith and love which are in Christ Jesus." Paul reminded Timothy to hold "the healthy words." He had already spoken about this in 1 Timothy 6. As we have already seen, these healthy words are the words of the Lord Jesus in the New Testament plus the preaching of the Lord's apostles concerning such things as God becoming flesh and the mystery of godliness. Paul charged

Timothy to hold these words. This proves that at that time some believers were already not holding these words. This is a very serious matter.

Second Timothy 1:14 says, "Guard the good deposit through the Holy Spirit who dwells in us." This is the Lord's commission to the apostles. It is also the apostles' charge to the believers. We have to deposit the Lord's healthy words, including the riches of life in the Lord's words, into our being, like we deposit money in the bank. Verse 15 says, "This you know, that all who are in Asia turned away from me." Paul was sitting in his prison in Rome. How could believers far away in the province of Asia have turned away from him? This proves that what the Asian believers were turning away from was not Paul's person but his ministry. The "me" here does not refer to Paul's person. It refers to his teaching. When we come to Revelation 2 and 3, we find the Lord writing to the seven churches in Asia, and the first letter was to the church in Ephesus. This proves that it was the church in Ephesus who took the lead to forsake Paul's ministry and teaching. This is the background of the writing of the second Epistle to Timothy.

THE PRESENT VISION AND PRACTICE

The burden in this chapter is not to expound the Epistles to Timothy but to continue from the previous chapter to speak on our present vision and practice.

The Problem Created
by the Ministry of Spirituality in the West

First, let us fellowship a little about our history. In 1955 Brother Austin-Sparks was invited for the first time to come to Taiwan. In 1957 he came for the second time. During the second time, he raised a crucial issue. He thought that the way we were taking was good in every matter except one. The one thing he considered to be seriously wrong and absolutely intolerable was the ground of the church. In other words, it was the practice of the church. While he was alive, he was the only one on the whole earth who could echo what we saw concerning spiritual life principles. He echoed what we saw, and we responded to what he saw. At that time the rejection he faced in the West was more severe than the rejection we faced in the East. In the entire Western world he was the only one who saw the principles of life, and he was the only one who spoke on the deeper truths of life. Almost no one accepted his teaching. In the East we also spoke on these deep matters. Hence, on the side of life principles, we held the same view. But on the side of church practice and church ground, we could not fellowship with each other. At that time we saw that the church ground cannot be separated from church practice. Without the ground there can be no practice. In order to have the practice, there must be the ground. However, he did not agree with the matter of the church ground, and he did not agree with that kind of church practice.

From 1937 to 1938, Brother Watchman Nee visited a number of countries in Europe and stayed there for over a year and a half. Most of the time he stayed in London with Brother Sparks. After he returned to China, he cabled me immediately to join him in Shanghai. At that time he called together a special fellowship meeting and reported to us in detail his fellowship with Brother Sparks in London. At the end he said that in almost every aspect they were in harmony with each other and echoed each other. The only exception was the practice of the church, which they could not get through in their fellowship. Brother Nee was somewhat sympathetic about the matter. He felt that in England the Brethren had spoiled the matter of church practice for over a hundred years. Because of this, most seekers of the Lord were unwilling to talk about the subject. Brother Nee sympathized with their frustrations and spoke to us in this way, but he also pointed out that this was exactly where the problem between Brother Sparks and us lay.

Inviting the Ministry of Spirituality from the West

After we heard Brother Nee's fellowship, we asked why we should not invite Brother Sparks to come and visit us, since Brother Nee spoke so highly of him. Brother Nee answered in a wise way: "The time has not come." At that time we did not quite understand what he meant. About fifteen years later, in 1954, our work in Taiwan was very much blessed by the Lord.

At that time a brother visited England and America and met with Brother Sparks. After his visit, he wrote three letters, one to Manila, one to Hong Kong, and one to Taipei, highly promoting Brother Sparks. He said that Brother Sparks was a spiritual giant and that he had a strong burden to come to the Far East to witness for the Lord.

In the first part of 1955, I was conducting the life-study training in Taipei. Brothers Chang Yu-lan and Chang Wu-cheng took the letter and showed it to me. After I read the letter, I considered a little. Then I told them that for many years we had learned a certain thing before the Lord: In knowing a person we should not look at the big matters but at the small matters. It is not very easy for a person to expose his flaws in the big things; the problems are always with the small things. Brother Sparks published a bimonthly magazine called "A Witness and a Testimony." In the January 1955 issue there was a column acknowledging the Christmas cards that he had received from readers. His magazine was altogether on spiritual subjects, yet there was such an acknowledgment. This was a small point. By the Lord's leading, we had completely dropped the celebration of Christmas, but Brother Sparks, whom we had always respected so much, published an acknowledgment thanking his readers for Christmas cards. From this small matter I could tell that there must still be some distance between him and us. If we were to invite him to come, it would be hard to guarantee that there would be no friction between us; perhaps the better thing to do would be to keep our distance and remain cordial to each other.

At that time the two elders agreed with what I said, but two weeks later, they said, "Brother Lee, we feel that on the spiritual side, we still need the spiritual help from Brother Sparks." The phrase *spiritual help* made it hard for me to say no to them. Since the brothers had felt that the small differences did not matter and that they needed spiritual help, how could I insist on not inviting him? I then suggested that if we were to invite him, it would be better not to bring up the subject of church practice, because Brother Nee had discussed this matter in detail with Brother Sparks already and had not been able to get through. The two Brothers Chang agreed and said, "We will only receive the spiritual help from him." I then drafted the letter in English myself. The Taipei brothers signed it and sent it to Hong Kong and Manila for their signatures. In this way, Brother Sparks came.

The Problem Brought About by the Practice

At the end of 1955 Brother Sparks came for the first time. He restricted his speakings to spiritual subjects. The messages helped many people. Everyone was happy and decided to invite him to come again. In the spring of 1957, he came again at our invitation, but this time it was different. He told us clearly about his feelings. After visiting for about a month, one morning we asked him to have a time of fellowship with the hundred or more co-workers that we had. One brother among us took the lead to ask, "Brother Sparks, you have been staying with us for some time, and you have observed our situation. What is your feeling about us?" As soon as I heard this, I knew right away that this brother had dissenting thoughts within him. It turned out that my feeling was correct. Right after this brother asked the question, Brother Sparks replied, "The last time I came, I did have some feelings, but I was determined not to say anything. I was waiting for another opportunity to come again to speak about them." Later I found out that this dissenting one was echoing Brother Sparks. He took the initiative to ask that question in order to provide Brother Sparks the opportunity to speak what he had prepared.

The first thing that Brother Sparks disagreed with was the way we conducted the bread-breaking meeting. He thought that our bread-breaking meeting was too disorderly. There was no proper order. One person could call a hymn, and another could pray. I did not say much about this because I was the translator. However, I will speak in detail about the second matter with which he did not agree. You have to realize that if one's vision is not clear, he can be very spiritual, but he can become quite confused in certain matters. The second thing that Brother Sparks mentioned showed that he was somewhat confused. He said, "Please tell me why the brothers among you who are in the military service put on their uniform cap even before they leave the meeting hall?" At that time we had many brothers among us who were in the military. They all came to the meetings dressed in military uniforms. After the meetings they would put on their caps and fellowship with the brothers and sisters in the meeting hall. When Brother Sparks saw this, he began to criticize.

At the time this happened, one brother answered Brother Sparks, saying, "According to the Chinese tradition, a soldier does not take off his cap when he is standing up, whether or not he is inside a building. These brothers remove their caps when they sit down for the meetings in accordance with the biblical teaching about not covering their head, but when the announcement is made that the meeting is dismissed, they put their cap back on." When Brother Sparks heard this, right away his countenance changed. He asked, "Are you here to keep the tradition, or are you here to keep the Bible?" When I heard this, I was not too happy inside. I realized that he was wrong. It was he who was following the Western tradition and not we who were disobeying the Bible. The Bible says that when a man prays or teaches, he should not cover his head (1 Cor. 11:4, 7), but it does not say that a man cannot put on his cap inside a house. To take off the cap inside a building is a Western tradition. Brother Sparks was imposing on us a tradition that Western unbelievers keep.

I did not have any prejudice against Brother Sparks. Before that day, I supported that elderly brother almost a hundred percent. He did render us quite an amount of help, and he also received some help from us. For a long time we communicated with one another and fellowshipped with one another, but from that day onward, I became alarmed. First of all, for him to say such a word lowered his spiritual ministry. Why did he have to touch such outward matters? At his invitation I went to London in 1958 and met with his group for four weeks. Their bread-breaking meeting lasted for an hour. During that whole time Brother Sparks took the lead. At the beginning he took the lead to pray, to call a hymn, and to speak. Afterwards everyone prayed for about ten minutes. At a certain point, he would break the bread and give it to the congregation. He would first give it to the seven deacons; then the seven deacons would distribute it to the others. After everyone had the bread in his hand, Brother Sparks would say, "Now we can eat." Only after he had announced this, was anyone allowed to eat. After the eating, they did the same with the distribution and drinking of the cup. At the end he stepped in and monopolized the meeting again by announcing, "Now the time for public worship is over," which meant that no one could do anything anymore. This was his way. It is no wonder that he considered our bread-breaking meeting to be somewhat disorganized.

Brother Sparks came to our meetings and started questioning such practices among us as the breaking of bread. He even touched on such insignificant matters as the donning of military caps. Was it not too much for him to touch such matters? These were traces that gave us a hint that his way and our way could not be reconciled because what we saw was different.

Defending the Ground of the Church

Recently I have felt the importance of the one accord. As long as we have different views on a minor point, we cannot have the one accord. This is why in this training, right from the start, I spoke about the vision in the Lord's recovery. I believe all the brothers and sisters love the Lord, and all of you want to be in one accord, but if our vision is not up-to-date, it is impossible for us to be one. Concerning Brother Sparks, I could never have dreamed that a spiritual ministry as high as his would touch upon and even seriously meddle with minor things. It was really not worth it. I kept all these things in my heart and did not tell anyone, because I did not want to ruin the atmosphere there. At that time over five hundred co-workers from all over the island were together. Every morning we were under the training and his ministry. I needed to maintain a good situation.

One evening we had another fellowship with Brother Sparks. The atmosphere was a little tense, and no one knew what to say. We thought perhaps we would fellowship a little about something related to spiritual principles. Suddenly a brother asked, "Brother Sparks, suppose here in Taipei there are five assemblies that meet in the Lord's name. Please tell us which one is right and which one is wrong, or are they all wrong?" As soon as I heard this, something jumped up in alarm within me. I knew that this would lead to trouble. Yet I had to translate what he said. Brother Sparks was well prepared for such a question. He said, "None is right and none is wrong; everything is relative." Another brother was quite stirred up, and he and the first brother together asked, "Relative to what?" Brother Sparks immediately answered, "Relative to the measure of Christ. Those who have a greater measure of Christ are more right; those who have a lesser measure of Christ are less right; and those who do not have any measure of Christ are not right." All the brothers became very agitated. I was the translator, but I had to somewhat calm them down.

The third time we gathered together with Brother Sparks, we were still on this subject. In the previous two meetings, I remained quite neutral and served only as the translator. This time I felt that I could not be neutral anymore. No one was speaking then, and I opened my mouth. I said, "For the last few times we were together we have been talking about the matter of the church and the church ground. Brother Sparks has told us that none is absolutely right, and none is absolutely wrong; how much one is right depends on the measure of Christ he has." I did not appear to be stirred up, but I turned to a brother from Denmark and said to him in a calm voice, "Brother, let me ask you a question. God ordained that the children of Israel would be taken captive in Babylon for seventy years, after which they would return to their homeland and would rebuild the temple upon its original foundation. Suppose a very influential prophet would rise up at that time and tell the people that it did not matter whether or not one returned to Jerusalem. Suppose he would say, 'See? Daniel is such a spiritual person, but he did not return to Jerusalem. Therefore, it does not matter whether or not one returns, as long as he is spiritual.' I would ask all of you here if this is right or wrong." Brother Sparks was an intelligent man. He knew that I was reacting to his word about the spiritual measure. I explained further: "Daniel had the greatest spiritual measure of his time; in today's terms, we would say that his measure of Christ was the highest. The reason why he did not return was that the time had not come for him to go. Around the time the Israelites were returning, he died. He could not go while he was living, yet his heart was toward Jerusalem. He knelt down three times a day and prayed with an open window toward Jerusalem. During his time with us here, at least a few times our Brother Sparks has highly recommended Dr. F. B. Meyer. I have read Dr. Meyer's books and have received some help from him. But all of us know that Brother Meyer is still in the denominations, that is, in the so-called 'organized Christianity' that our Brother Sparks condemns in his messages. Since Dr. Meyer still remains in organized Christianity, the very organization which Brother Sparks condemns, can we say that he is right in the matter of the church just because his spiritual stature is high?"

I continued, "For over three hundred years, all those who have sought after the inner life have received help from Madame Guyon. She should be regarded as a person with a great measure of Christ. As far as the spiritual stature of Christ is concerned, probably none among us can match hers. But Madame Guyon, a person with such a spiritual stature of Christ, still remained in Catholicism. Today any Christian who is enlightened at all would condemn Catholicism, yet Madame Guyon whom we respect so much never left the Catholic Church. We cannot say that just because her spiritual stature was high that she was right in the matter of the church."

Finally I said, "These examples prove to us that it is one thing to be spiritual and it is another thing to have the proper ground of the church. Spirituality has to do with our personal condition. The ground of the church, on the other hand, is a corporate ground; it is the corporate standing that we take. Not everyone who left Babylon to return to Jerusalem was a spiritual person. Neither was everyone who remained in Babylon necessarily unspiritual. In fact, among those who returned, we find many who were not that spiritual, because some had married Gentile wives. However, as far as their ground was concerned, they were approved by God. With such a ground they could build the temple. No matter how poor their situation was, their ground was still the right ground. When the temple was built, God's glory filled the house." I then made the following conclusion: "Today in pursuing the Lord, we have to take care of both aspects. Spirituality has to do with our condition, while the ground has to do with our stand. A man cannot be right only in his condition; he must also be right in his stand and position. Whether or not a person has a justifiable position is based not so much on his condition as on the ground he takes. No matter how spiritual a person was, if he remained in Babylon and stood on the ground of captivity, he was wrong. On the other hand, no matter how poor and confused the returned captives were, they stood on the proper ground which God had ordained for them and which their forefathers had left to them. Their approval was based on their ground and not on their personal condition. Of course their confused situation did not please the Lord. This is why God raised up Ezra to teach them the law to enlighten and rebuke them; as a result, they wept, repented, and confessed their sins. At any rate, we cannot despise the returned captives' ground just because their spiritual condition was poor. Nor can we justify the ground of those remaining in Babylon just because they were spiritual."

OUR VISION NEEDING TO MATCH THE AGE

In the previous chapter we said that God gave men a vision even in the Old Testament age. We cannot say that those who remain in the Old Testament visions do not have any vision at all. Yet their visions are not up-to-date; they do not match the age. In the New Testament, after the four Gospels we have the book of Acts. After Acts we have the early letters of Paul. Paul went into prison, was released, was imprisoned again, and then was martyred. By that time, he had written his Epistles. All of them concerned God's visions. About thirty years after his martyrdom, around A.D. 90, the aged John wrote the book of Revelation. It also was a book of visions. We can say that the entire Bible from Genesis to Revelation is a record of visions. Throughout the ages there were many saints who loved the Lord and who feared the Lord, but we cannot say that they all had the vision that matched their age. Some, like Gamaliel, were still stuck in the Old Testament age. I believe Apollos somewhat belongs to this category of people, because Acts 18 says that he was powerful in expounding the Scriptures (v. 24). He knew the Old Testament well, but he did not know the four Gospels; he only knew the baptism of John (v. 25b). His vision only went that far. He did not see any further vision after John the Baptist.

The Case of James

In Acts 15 we find James becoming the leading brother among those in the church in Jerusalem. Although he was a man in the New Testament, he had one foot in the New Testament and the other foot in the Old Testament. His two feet were standing on two "boats," and his two hands were holding on to two "oars." He was very pious and he feared God very much. History tells us that he was so pious that the skin of his knees grew coarser than an elephant's skin from kneeling. It was his piety that attracted many to the Lord. It was also his piety that made him the chief apostle among those in the church in Jerusalem. However, although he was spiritual, he did not have an adequate vision. History tells us that the Pharisees and priests thought that James was for Judaism. They even gathered together the Jews and the Christians around Jerusalem and asked James to speak to them. However, James feared the Lord very much, and he spoke on the New Testament on that occasion. This upset the Jews, and they killed him on the spot. This is how James was martyred. It is hard to say whether James's martyrdom was something pleasing to the Lord. How could God reward him for his ambiguous condition? All we can say is, "Only the Lord knows." Although James was much more advanced than Gamaliel, he also did not have the vision that matched the age.

The Case of Barnabas

Then there was Barnabas. He was the one who ushered Paul into his apostolic ministry (Acts 11:25-26). In Acts 13, when the Holy Spirit commissioned him and Paul to the ministry, he was the leader between the two. Halfway through their journey, however, there was a turn in the ministry. When the critical time came for someone to speak for God, Barnabas had nothing to say, and Paul took his place. From that day onward, Paul became the leader. In other words, the vision and the revelation shifted to Paul; they were no longer with Barnabas. At the end of chapter fifteen, the two of them contended, and they parted from each other. From that time onward, the Bible does not mention anything further about Barnabas's fellowship and work. This means that Barnabas disappeared from the stage of God's move at that time. He no longer played a role on that stage. Although he was still in the New Testament, the vision he saw was not adequate.

The Case of Apollos

In Acts 18 Apollos appeared on the scene. He was a person partly in the Old Testament and partly in the New Testament. As we have seen, he went to Ephesus and the church in Ephesus first received help from him. In the end, Apollos's work dominated Ephesus by virtue of its early arrival. Once Apollos's seed took root in the church in Ephesus, it was hard to eradicate it. We can detect through various hints that the cause of Ephesus's decline was its failure to rid itself of Apollos's seed. From the standpoint of the New Testament, that teaching was a different teaching; it was a different doctrine. The work of Apollos left a lasting mark of different teachings on the church in Ephesus. For this reason, Paul was always concerned about the church in Ephesus, as evidenced by Acts 20.

THE CHURCHES' DECLINE
THROUGH FORSAKING THE APOSTLES' TEACHING

From the time of Paul's first imprisonment to the time he was imprisoned again was a period of about three years. During that period he charged Timothy to remain in Ephesus to take care of the church because there was a problem there. Some were teaching differently. During Paul's second imprisonment, he wrote the second Epistle to Timothy to tell him that all the churches in Asia had forsaken his ministry. Here we can trace the source of the churches' decline. The cause for the churches' decline was the forsaking of the apostles' teaching; they forsook the apostles' ministry. Because of this forsaking, the teaching of

Balaam, the teaching of the Nicolaitans, and the teaching of Jezebel (Rev. 2—3) crept into the church one by one. These three kinds of teachings represent all the heresies. When the church departs from the apostles' teaching, all kinds of doctrines invade the church. This is very clear.

THE ULTIMATE CONSUMMATION
OF THE DIVINE REVELATION

About thirty years later, the aged John wrote the book of Revelation. After he finished writing about the New Jerusalem in the new heaven and new earth, God's visions were complete. At the end of Revelation, which is the end of the entire Bible, there is the warning against any further addition or deletion. All the visions of God have been completed. After the book of Revelation was completed, three hundred years went by until in A.D. 397, at the Council of Carthage, the authority of the entire canon of the holy writings, including the books of Revelation and Hebrews, was recognized. In A.D. 325 when Emperor Constantine convened the Council of Nicaea, the books of Revelation and Hebrews still had not been recognized as part of the canon. These two books occupy a pivotal position in the vision concerning God's New Testament economy. Hence, the creed produced at the Council of Nicaea did not include the revelation revealed in these two books. Today many Protestant and Catholic groups recite the Nicene Creed every Sunday in their services. While I was in the West fighting for the truth concerning the Triune God, I told people, "The creed that you hold is defective, for it does not say anything about the seven Spirits." They had nothing to say in response.

THE BASIS OF THE ONE ACCORD

By A.D. 397, the entire Bible was recognized. Today this holy Word before us is full of visions. Whether or not we can come up to the standard of these visions depends entirely on our understanding of the visions contained in these sixty-six books. During the first sixteen hundred years of church history, countless numbers of lovers of the Lord were raised up. Unfortunately all these lovers of the Lord, all these servants of God, were not able to be in one accord. The reason for this is that the visions they saw were all different. Some only saw the vision of the four Gospels. They liked it, and they faithfully adhered to that vision, but they did not advance any further. Some advanced a little and saw the vision of Acts. Spontaneously they became different from the first group, and they discovered that they could not fellowship with the first group. Other people advanced to the different visions recorded in the different Epistles, and similarly they held different views from the previous groups. Throughout the last sixteen centuries, many lovers of the Lord were raised up, yet they were not able to be in one accord. The reason is not that there was sin or evil among them, but that the vision each held was different in degree. Each remained in the degree to which they saw the various visions. Because the degree of the visions they saw was different, spontaneously there was no one accord.

In the nineteenth century, Hudson Taylor saw a vision. He felt that he should go to China to preach the gospel. You cannot say that his vision was wrong. You can only say that his vision was not up to the standard of the age. During the past three decades, we lost the one accord a number of times in Taiwan. The case with Brother Austin-Sparks was one example of such a time. Can you say that he did not love the Lord or that he was not spiritual? Even today I still recommend his books. Some of them are indeed worthwhile reading. However, he did not see what Brother Nee led us to see in the Lord's recovery. Needless to say, all our differences were not caused by the flesh but by the difference in our visions. In 1958, there were some aspiring and promising young people who were saved and perfected through my ministry. I entrusted to them the crucial works on the island of Taiwan, including hall three of the church in Taipei and the churches in Taichung, Chiayi, Tainan, and Kaoshung. They became proud, and through Brother Spark's influence, they decided to no longer speak about the ground of the church but to speak only about the fullness of Christ, the full Christ. They boldly proclaimed that they had seen a vision. At that time, the one accord was truly lost.

Although Brother Sparks was spiritual, he limited himself to the scope of his vision. His problem was that he was unwilling to see more. Moreover, he considered all those who saw something different to be wrong. He tried all he could to annul the "ground," which was recovered among us. He told me personally in a meeting that he had been speaking for decades, but in his whole life he had not found one place with such a good audience. He also discussed with me the possibility of moving to Taiwan to set up a ministry station. In the end, however, he and we were still not the same. The reason for this is that our visions were different.

THE PRESENT VISION OF THE LORD'S RECOVERY

What then is our vision? A young brother once said, "Brother Nee used to talk about the cross, but we do not talk about it anymore." This is a shortsighted remark. Who says that we no longer speak about the dealing of the cross? If you read the messages on the New Jerusalem, you will see that in order to become the gates of pearl we have to pass through the Lord's death. We have to enjoy the secretion of the Lord's resurrection life through His death. Only then can we become the pearls. Every one of the nineteen items in the book *The Experience of Life* involves dealings that have to do with the cross. We need to speak about the dealing of the cross, but we should not make this truth our limitation or our issue. In the West some people emphasize tongue-speaking. We do not oppose tongue-speaking, but if someone emphasizes tongue-speaking to the point of strongly promoting it, it becomes a great damage. One may do this out of harmless zeal, but if his listeners receive his speaking and enlarge upon it, it will bring a problem to the church. We have to remember that the vision we have received does not concern itself with such small matters. This is not the focus of our vision.

What is our vision? Our vision is that God so loved the world that He gave His Son to die for us to redeem us, the sinners, in order that we can have the life of Christ and be regenerated by Him to be God's children, enjoying the riches of the Triune God to become the Body of Christ. In practice, the Body is expressed as the local churches in various localities, practicing the Body life in a practical and proper way. This Body, the church of God, is the focus of God's economy.

In the theology of the early church fathers there was such a term as "economy," but in the Lord's recovery, during the period when we were in mainland China, we did not use this term. It was twenty years ago that I first picked up this term in Taiwan, but it was only two years ago that we saw the entire New Testament economy of God. At the same time we saw the mingling of God and man and the divine dispensing, which is the Triune God dispensing all His riches in Christ as the Spirit into us to constitute us the Body of Christ. This is God's economy.

During the past few centuries, no one saw God's economy. Even if some did see it, no one spoke about it. No one spoke about the mingling of God and man, and no one spoke about the divine dispensing. Some spoke about sanctification, but that speaking was somewhat ambiguous. From the Bible we see that sanctification is of three stages. There is separating sanctification, positional sanctification, and dispositional sanctification. Dispositional sanctification is transformation, and transformation includes the dealing and breaking of the cross. But even the inner-life Christians, including those attending the Keswick conferences and the many spiritual giants who have written on the subject of the spiritual life, did not clearly explain what transformation is. The teaching of transformation is an item which is characteristic to the Lord's recovery.

The vision that the Lord has given to His recovery is an all-inclusive one. It includes the economy of God, the mingling of God and man, the dispensing of the Divine Trinity, and the believers' salvation in Christ, including God's selection, calling, regeneration, sanctification, renewing, transformation, conformation, and glorification. In the history of the development of Christian doctrine, this entire set of truths finds its full recovery only among us. Such truths as selection, calling, regeneration, sanctification, renewing, transformation, conformation, and glorification were not recovered much before us, and the recovery of these truths will not increase much after us. This set of truths has found its full recovery among us.

THE PROBLEM AND DANGER OF A VISION
NOT MATCHING THE AGE

The problem among us is that some are bound by the little experience and vision they have. Some have said that Brother Lee is now different from Brother Nee. This is a remark made not only by those outside the Lord's recovery or by some who have left us, but by some who are still among us. Actually, if there is anyone on this earth who knows Brother Nee, I must be that one. He fellowshipped with me all that he had seen, and I received tremendous help from him. If anyone says that my work is different from Brother Nee's, he is an outsider with regard to the vision. Of course, because of the lack of opportunity on his part, Brother Nee did not develop the vision as far as I have. We may use the Recovery Version of the New Testament as an example. I spent twelve years day after day writing the footnotes, yet what I wrote was nothing more than what Brother Nee had sown earlier. I can only say that the seed has sprouted and grown, although, of course, it has not grown to the fullest. I ask the Lord to give me more years so that I can develop this seed within me. If the Lord would give me another twelve years to rewrite the life-study messages, I will have another set of life-studies. It will not be different, but it will be new. If anyone thinks that I am different from Brother Nee, it is because such a person has not come up to the standard of the vision of the age!

I would like the co-workers, the elders, and all the churches in the Lord's recovery to realize that today we have not changed. If we are different in any way from others, it is because we hold to all the visions of the Bible, from the first vision of Adam in Genesis to the ultimate, consummate one in Revelation. If anyone sees only a part of this entire vision and condemns us for being different, it is not merely because we are different from them; it is because they do not have the vision that matches the age.

We cannot blame those whose vision does not match the age for doing what they are doing. James was very pious. We cannot criticize him for his piety, yet he did not have the vision that matched the age. In the end he not only destroyed himself, but he destroyed the work of God and brought trouble to all the saints in the land of Judea. Because of his inertia and reluctance, the Roman prince Titus marched with his army in A.D. 70 and ransacked Jerusalem. The temple was destroyed, and not one stone was left on top of another. Josephus the historian told us the tragedy of the whole story. Many Christians were killed. Even children were murdered. Who would have wished that the whole matter end this way? However, God was forced to do this. If God had not done this, the result would have been even more unmanageable. Christianity would have become entirely mixed with Judaism. Faced with such a murky situation, God had to step in to clear the atmosphere. The fact that Jerusalem was burned to the ground and that thousands of people were killed was altogether James's fault. This is not a small thing. This is what the Chinese mean by "off by a fraction of an inch, missed by a thousand miles." One faulty step resulted in the loss of tens of thousands of lives. History bears a tragic testimony to this.

Today the Lord indeed has been merciful to His recovery. Within a short period of sixty years, He has brought us to the ultimate consummation of all the visions. I hope that all of us will seriously study the messages that we have published, especially those in the *Elders' Training* and *Truth Lessons* series. If you study them well, you will have the full view; you will see the vision that the Lord has given us in His recovery, and you will realize what is the ultimate consummation of all the visions—the New Jerusalem. Within this ultimate consummation everything is included, such as gospel preaching, loving the Lord, the dealing and breaking of the cross, the resurrection life, and the outpouring of the Holy Spirit.

Unfortunately, today on the earth, when believers see a little revelation in the New Testament, they begin to think quite highly of themselves. They become very zealous concerning that one point that they see. So naturally they think that our actions and words are too extreme. There is no doubt that many Christian groups are very busy on the earth today, but not only are they not able to be one with us; they are not able to be one with each other. They cannot be one mainly because they have different visions; they see different things. This difference is a difference in degree, although the basis is still the same. We have the same Bible, the same God, and the same Savior, and we have received the same Spirit and the same salvation. We all believe in the blood of the Lord, and we all share the same faith, but any further advance beyond this basis ends in differences. Some advance only a few steps and then stop; others advance a few steps more; and some advance even further. We thank the Lord for giving us the same basis. We are all saved, and we all have God's life and nature. We all have the same standing. However, while the Holy Spirit is moving on, we may remain where we are. The minute the Holy Spirit moves on, some decide to follow while others decide to stay. The more the Holy Spirit moves on, the fewer there are who follow Him. In the end, we are the only ones left who have followed Him all the way.

ANSWERING THE LORD'S CALL AND FOLLOWING THE PRESENT VISION TO BE THE OVERCOMERS

Faced with such a situation, what should we do? Thank the Lord that at the end of the Bible there is the call to the overcomers. Although the seven churches in Revelation 2 and 3 had degraded and their condition was poor, the Lord still recognized them as churches. The Lord did not call the overcomers to leave the seven churches. Why? Because their ground was still the right ground. They were not meeting as many churches in one locality but as one church in each locality. Although the condition of Thyatira was poor, it was still one church in one locality. Its ground was still the right ground. It was corrupt, and its condition was poor, but its ground was still the right ground. This can be compared to a member of a family. Whether the family is a good one or a poor one, that person still belongs to the family. If he separates himself to start another family and changes his name, he is splitting up the family. According to his condition, he may be very good, moral, and educated. However, as for his standing, his ground, he has caused a division. In the same way, we can say that Thyatira was poor beyond measure, yet the Lord did not ask anyone to leave the church in Thyatira, because it was still standing on the proper ground. The Lord instead called some to be overcomers in the midst of that situation. Today's situation is the same. Many have seen the initial vision, and they are satisfied with what they have seen, but they should not stop there. We have to follow the Holy Spirit, and we have to go on, but the more we go on, the fewer there will be who follow. Hence, it is not true that we refuse to be one with others. The truth of the matter is that they will not follow. We are not only following, but we are practicing what we have seen and what we follow, which is the dispensing of the Triune God, the mingling of God and man, to become the Body of Christ to be the manifestation of the Triune God. In the process of becoming this, we experience regeneration, sanctification, renewing, transformation, conformation, and glorification.

THE PRESENT PRACTICE IN THE LORD'S RECOVERY— PREACHING THE GOSPEL, NOURISHING THE NEW ONES, TEACHING THE TRUTH, AND BUILDING UP THE CHURCH

In our practice we have to take care of the increase. First we have to spread the high gospel and bring people to salvation. Next we have to build up the home meetings and nourish the new ones. Then we have to build up the small groups and teach the truth. Finally we have to edify and perfect the new ones to be the same as we are, practicing the Body life in all the local churches for the Lord to gain a full-grown, mature Body. These are the four things that we have to attain in our practice. If we all see this clearly, we will be in one accord. We cannot stay in the past; there is no future in that kind of standing. That vision and practice is short. With only that vision there is no preaching of the gospel and no teaching of the truth; there is only the bearing of the cross, the dealing and breaking of the cross. What kind of future will this narrow view afford us? I am very clear about the responsibility that the Lord has given me. More or less I am a leading one, and I have to bear great responsibility for the things I say and do, because they affect hundreds, even tens of thousands of people. In the future I have to give an account to the Lord. For this very reason I have observed the situation very much. Some emphasize the preaching of the cross, but there is not much practice with them. When they want to lose their temper, they still lose their temper. They do not preach the gospel, they do not nourish and perfect others, and they do not pursue after the truth. The cross is just a doctrine to them. We do not care for mere doctrines. We have to see the vision. As we have seen, the vision that matches the age is the vision that extends all the way from Genesis to Revelation.

Now we need to consider the proper practice. Matthew 24:14 says, "This gospel of the kingdom will be preached in the whole inhabited earth for a testimony to all the nations, and then the end will come." This means that we have to do everything we can today to spread the gospel. We should spend every cent and every drop of our sweat, tears, and blood on the gospel. Only this will satisfy the Lord and take care of His gospel. The little island of Taiwan has twenty million people, but there are only five hundred thousand Christians. Are we sitting still, not willing to be on fire for the gospel? If we are, how can we give an account to the Lord? I believe one day, when we stand before the judgment seat of the Lord, He will ask us, "You have been in Taiwan for so long. What was your attitude towards My gospel?" He will tell us that He was not a hard Master, that He had given us a talent. But how did we use it, and how much did we use it? How many people did we bring to the Lord? How many people did we nourish and care for? How many people did we teach? In the future we will have to answer these questions one by one.

Matthew 24 and 25 show us that one day we will have to stand before the Lord and give an account item by item. I admit that my responsibility is greater than yours. I will have to stand before Him also to give an account of myself, but I cannot give an account on your behalf. Today you have risen up and have responded to my leading, and I thank and praise the Lord for this. I worship the Lord for you, but you have to be clear that you are not following me. You are following this ultimate and completed vision, and you are spreading the gospel according to the Lord's commandment. No one can say that he does not know how to preach the gospel. Matthew

28:19 says, "Go therefore and disciple all the nations." This commandment is to all the believers. The Bible has never said that some are exempt from preaching the gospel. If we are faithful to the Lord in the matter of the gospel, and if we are diligent, the number of believers in the churches will greatly increase in a country as densely populated as Taiwan, but if we do not do anything, we will have nothing to say when we face the Lord.

Those who are sitting here today are either co-workers, elders, or full-timers who are learning to serve the Lord. Please consider calmly: If you cannot save one or two people within a year in an island as populous as Taiwan, how are you going to give an account to the Lord when you see Him? If each of us brings one to the Lord in a year, in a short time we will reach the goal of gospelizing Taiwan, but if we all hold back our energy, how can we gospelize this country? In the parable of Matthew 20, the householder went out and said to the idle workmen, "Why have you been standing here all the day idle?" (v. 6). All those who do not participate in the gospel move, even if they are pursuing "spirituality" and are knowledgeable in the truth, are idle in the eyes of the Lord. Today when we speak about the one accord, we are not speaking about a certain method that we have to practice. We are saying that we should be attuned to the Lord's heart. The Lord's heart is that we enter the vineyard and labor for His gospel. If we are attuned to the Lord's heart, and if we dispense the Triune God to others, imparting to them the Lord's life so that they become His members and are constituted to be His Body as His full expression, then spontaneously we will be in one accord.

THE PRESENT NEED—BEING IN ONE ACCORD
AND BEING FAITHFUL IN COORDINATION

The preaching of the gospel is the first step in the spreading. Following this we have to have home meetings and the nourishing of the new believers. We also have to build up the small groups and teach the truth. Finally we have to have the practical manifestation of the Body life. These four things must become the "family tradition" among the churches in the Lord's recovery. In order to develop this "tradition," we must have the same view and the one accord. This is why I have presented to you the matter of the ultimate and completed vision. Today we should no longer emphasize different ways. We should not have any different leadings. We are all in the Lord's recovery, and we all have seen today's concluded vision. Even if some cannot follow and do not see clearly, they should not say anything. As long as they follow, they will get the blessing. The sons of Noah did not see the vision that he saw, yet they were in one accord with their father. They closely followed him, and they were saved in the same way that their father was saved. Peter was also one who blindly followed the Lord. He did not know anything. He only knew that the vision was with the Lord, and he followed. In the end he received the blessing.

If we have different emphases and different ways of doing things, our energy will be dissipated, and our faith will be weakened. We will lose the one accord, and our morale will be gone. However, if we are in one accord and we preach the gospel desperately, we will become hotter and hotter; our mutual burning will heighten our determination. Even the new ones will be brought into the proper function. We will have an invincible morale, and we will march over all obstacles. Wherever we go, we will more than conquer. This is what we must have today.

Do not ask why we did not do this ten years ago. Ten years ago we were not as clear as we are today about the way of the work. Thank the Lord that His leading is always progressive. If a child does not grow in ten years, he must be sick with some terrible illness. If I am still teaching the same thing as I did ten years ago, you may think that I have not grown. We are not changing our way. During the past twenty-three years that I was in America, I did not change my tone. Faced with all the oppositions and attacks, I stood firm on the truth. However, we are advancing and spreading. Today our work has to advance because the vision that the Lord has given us has advanced.